Helion & Company Limited
Unit 8 Amherst Business Centre
Budbrooke Road
Warwick
CV34 5WE
England
Tel. 01926 499 619
Email: info@helion.co.uk
Website: www.helion.co.uk
Twitter: @helionbooks
Visit our blog http://blog.helion.co.uk/

Text © Kevin Wright 2022
Photographs © as individually credited
Colour artwork © Tom Cooper and
    Anderson Subtil 2022
Maps drawn by George Anderson © Helion
    & Company 2022 and Tom Cooper 2022

Designed and typeset by Farr out
    Publications, Wokingham, Berkshire
Cover design Paul Hewitt, Battlefield Design
    (www.battlefield-design.co.uk)

ISBN 978-1-915070-69-2

British Library Cataloguing-in-Publication
    Data
A catalogue record for this book is available
    from the British Library

We always welcome receiving book
proposals from prospective authors.

CONTENTS

Note: In order to simplify the use of this book, all names, locations and geographic designations are as provided in *The Times World Atlas*, or other traditionally accepted major sources of reference, as of the time of described events or as cited in the sources consulted.

ABBREVIATIONS

AB	Air Base
ACAS (I)	Assistant Chief of the Air Staff (Intelligence) (RAF)
AFB	Air Force Base
AFSC	Air Force Systems Command
AFSPPF	Air Force Special Projects Production Facility
ALSS	Airborne Location Strike System
ARC	Ad-hoc Requirements Committee
Art	Article No, Lockheed allocated U-2 airframe number
ASARS	Advanced Synthetic Aperture Radar System
ATTG	Aerospace Technical Development and Training Group
BW	Biological Warfare
COMINT	Communications Intelligence
COMIREX	Committee on Imagery Requirements and Exploitation
COMOR	Committee on Overhead Reconnaissance
CW	Chemical Warfare
DCI	Director of Central Intelligence (CIA)
DPRK	Democratic People's Republic of Korea
ECCM	Electric Counter Counter Measures
EK	Eastman Kodak
ELINT	Electronic Intelligence
ETPS	Empire Test Pilots School
FAA	Federal Aviation Authority
FAS	Federation of American Scientists
GCI	Ground Control Intercept
GRC	Government of the Republic of China
HASP	High Altitude Sampling Programme
HMG	Her Majesty's Government
HTA	HT Automat
ICBM	Inter Continental Ballistic Missile
INS	Inertial Navigation System
IPIR	Initial Photographic Interpretation Report
IRBM	Intermediate-Range Ballistic Missile
JATO	Jet Assisted Take Off
JCS	Joint Chiefs of Staff
JIC	Joint Intelligence Committee (UK)
LOROP	Long Range Oblique Photography
LSO	Landing Signals Officer
MCP	Mission Coverage Plot
MoD	Ministry of Defence (UK)
NARA	National Archives and Records Administration
NAS	Naval Air Station
nm	nautical miles
NPIC	National Photographic Intelligence Centre
NRO	National Reconnaissance Office
NSA	National Security Agency
NSC	National Security Council
OBC	Optical Bar Camera
ORBAT	Order of Battle
OSA	Office of Special Activities (CIA)
PFIAB	President's Foreign Intelligence Advisory Board
PI	Photographic Interpreter
PID	Photographic Interpretation Division
PLA	People's Liberation Army

PoE	Point of Entry/Exit
PRC	People's Republic of China
RAE	Royal Aircraft Establishment
ROC	Republic of China
RTS	Reconnaissance Technical Squadron
SAC	Strategic Air Command
SAM	Surface-to-air Missile
SAR	Search and Rescue
SIGINT	Signals Intelligence (collective term for all forms of electronic signal collection)
SYERS	SENIOR YEAR Electro-Optical Reconnaissance System
TDY	Tour-of-duty
TELINT	Telemetry Intelligence
TNA	The National Archive (UK)
TRW	Tactical Reconnaissance Wing
URPIC	Temporary processing facilities deployed from Wiesbaden or Yakota
USAFE	US Air Force Europe
USAFSS	US Air Force Security Service
USIB	US Intelligence Board
WRSP	Weather Reconnaissance Squadron Provisional

Cryptonyms

AQUATONE	CIA U-2 programme up to April 1958
BLACK SHIELD	CIA A-12 deployments against North Vietnam in May 1967
CHALICE	CIA U-2 programme from April 1958
HBJAYWALK	Network for passing U-2 electronic communications
IDEALIST	CIA U-2 programme from May 1960
JACKSON	UK participation in CIA U-2 programme from October 1960
OLDSTER	UK participation in CIA U-2 programme from June 1958
RAZOR	ROC agreement with CIA for operation of U-2 programme
STBARNUM	CIA operations programme in Tibet
TACKLE	ROC participation in CIA U-2 programme from October 1960

INTRODUCTIONS AND ACKNOWLEDGEMENTS

Flying operationally from 1956, CIA U-2 overflights had concentrated on the USSR and Eastern Europe and flown many more missions over the Middle Eastern states. Overshadowing its considerable early achievements was the very public loss of Gary Powers, near Sverdlovsk, on 1 May 1960. Those U-2 operations up to 1960 are covered in Volume 1, of *We Were Never There*. This volume concentrates on operations, largely outside of Europe and the Middle East, up to 1974 when the CIA 'IDEALIST' programme terminated.

The story of CIA U-2 operations after 1960 is a considerably more complex one than the first five years. It lasted some 14 years. We start with Detachment C's early operations from Japan, moving on to Detachment H missions, mounted by the nationalist Chinese, from1961, under the project name TACKLE. Some of those overflights against the Lanzhou and Baotou nuclear facilities, the Shuang Cheng Tzu missile test centre and the epic flights to Lop Nor, are truly remarkable. The bravery of the Taiwanese pilots, who incurred such heavy losses, is sometimes overlooked. CIA U-2 operations over Cuba from 1960 until October 1962 are briefly covered. Detachment G, based at Edwards AFB, had a worldwide deployment role and during its existence operated from several locations across Asia and Europe. At times its rapid intercontinental agility was truly astonishing. Notable, was the development of an aerial refuelling capability for the U-2 and modifications to enable contingency operations from aircraft carriers. Although in many ways the various detachments worked independently, they were all components of the overarching IDEALIST project. Behind the scenes were bureaucratic battles about the CIA's continued role in airborne intelligence collection. Amongst all of this was the introduction of the new U-2R, a significantly more capable airframe, better suited to its changing role. The final chapter covers the last few years of CIA U-2 operations up to 1974 when the aircraft was handed over to the US Air Force.

Again, with this volume, I have attempted to provide an extensive account of the U-2's activities, primarily based on declassified Agency records, many still significantly redacted, to provide details of individual missions and operations. Many of the descriptions and maps used here from several of the individual missions discussed have not been available before. I hope to present you with a more operations-centred account of the U-2's remarkable achievements in CIA service.

It has proved enlightening to examine so much detailed material about this fascinating aircraft and the organisation behind it. Like so many things, to achieve this without the aid of others would have proved impossible. Therefore, my thanks go to retired USAF U-2 pilots, Lieutenant Colonels Bruce Jinneman and Rick Bishop, for helping me understand the workings of the early U-2s and for sharing their experiences flying the aircraft. My gratitude also to Joseph Caddell, Chris Pocock, Paul Lashmar, Paul Howard, Mick West, Akira Watanabe, Fred Willemsen, Brian Lockett, Robert Hopkins, Ralf Manteufel, Kevin Slade, the Center for Strategic and International Studies, US Air Force Historical Foundation, and the Center for the Study of National Reconnaissance, for kindly allowing me to use their images and help with other material. My special thanks again go to Dr Jason Ur for allowing me to borrow freely from his research.

1

EARLY ASIAN MISSIONS

When Gary Powers was shot down on 1 May 1960, it brought an abrupt halt to U-2 overflights. It also halted the many peripheral collection missions, flown by US Air Force and US Navy intelligence collection aircraft, for some months. It caused several allies to rethink their part in these operations.

When Detachments A and B had been reaching their peak in 1958–1959, flying missions over Eastern Europe, the Middle East and USSR, Asian and Far East operations were just gathering pace. After Mayday 1960, the emphasis shifted to Asia and the Far East. Soon a pattern of CIA U-2 operations developed across Asia that became far more complex and lasted much longer than those in Europe and the Middle East. To unfold the complexity of operations in Asia we start by stepping back a little and looking at the activities of Detachment C from 1956 to 1960.

Detachment C

Det C began training at the Watertown strip in Nevada during August 1956 and planned to deploy to the Far East. Its existence, from 1957 to 1960, was an unsettled one. Its original Alaskan base was useful for covering the USSR's northern and Far Eastern coastal areas, including Kamchatka. However, within this vast, largely empty space, apart from a few isolated airfields and what became the terminal missile range on Kamchatka, potential high priority areas of interest were pretty thin. The most important ones were further south, many within the People's Republic of China, but these required the use of airfields much closer to the target areas. Even obvious locations from which to launch overflights – Japan and Taiwan – presented substantial challenges.

Whilst training went ahead, basing problems delayed operational deployment. Yakota AB in Japan was the CIA's preference, but the USAF was determined to deny the Agency use of the airfield, planning to deploy its own high-level reconnaissance RB-57Ds there. The USAF offered possibilities of using a Korean base or Shemya, in the Aleutian Islands. The latter was particularly unsuitable with its severe climate. Shemya was a very important island airfield, used by the RC-135 'Cobra Ball' fleet from 1961 to 1994. They monitored the arrival of Soviet missile test warheads, fired at the Klyuchi range. Weather conditions were so treacherous that three RC-135s were lost in landing accidents at Shemya AB over the years. This was certainly not an airfield suitable for the much more delicate U-2. After a great deal of foot-dragging, the CIA was eventually afforded space at US Navy Air Facility Astugi, Japan, in early December 1956.

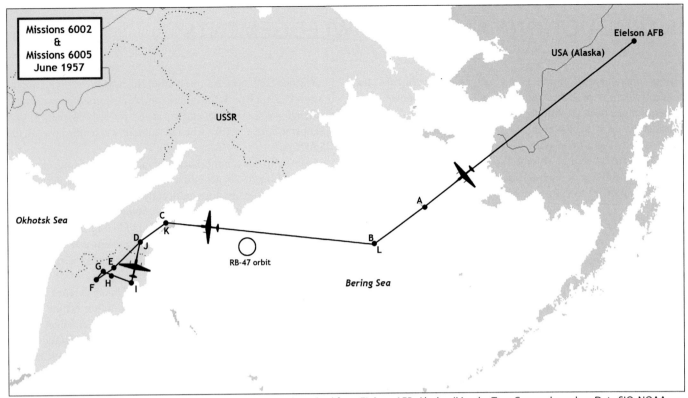

Missions 6002 & Missions 6005 June 1957

Early long range missions over the Kamchatka peninsula were launched from Eielson AFB, Alaska. (Map by Tom Cooper based on Data SIO, NOAA, USN, GEBCO and Landsat)

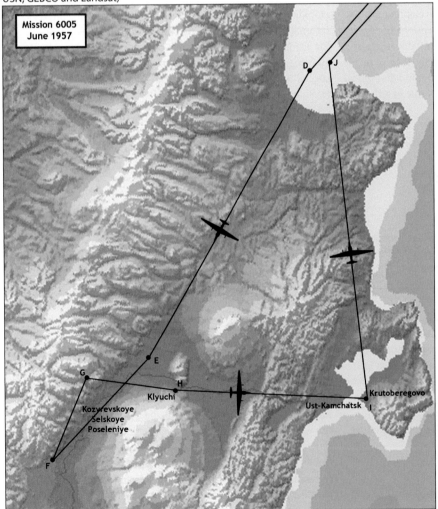

Mission 6005 June 1957

Missions 6002 and 6005 in June 1957 targeted the suspected terminal missile range at Klyuchi on Kamchatka. 6002 was severely hampered by cloud coverage. Re-flown on 19 and 20 June as Mission 6005, much better coverage was obtained. (Map by Tom Cooper based on Data SIO, NOAA, USN, GEBCO and Landsat)

The deteriorating relationship between the CIA and USAF, over Far East U-2 basing and operations was later characterised by Richard Bissell as descending from 'full and open support and partnership to one of increasing jurisdictional jealousy'.[1] Eisenhower was persuaded by Strategic Air Command (SAC) and agreed to a six RB-57D aircraft mission from Yakota on 11 December 1956. They split into two groups. One made a feint, whilst the other proceeded to fly directly over Vladivostock imaging the city, port and surrounding areas. The scale of the mission alerted Soviet air defences in the region and provoked a very detailed, robust Soviet protest. It specified precise times for the penetration stating that the good visibility: 'precluded any possibility of the loss of orientation by fliers during their flight'.[2] The immediate result of the Soviet protest was a 'by hand' order to Defence Secretary Wilson, Admiral Radford and John Foster Dulles from the president, prohibiting all further reconnaissance flights over Iron Curtain states.[3]

After some construction work required by the CIA was completed, their U-2s arrived at Astugi by 20 March 1957, under cover of being 'WRSP III'. However, that flawed December RB-57D flight significantly impacted plans for the U-2s' wider use. Their first operational mission saw them deployed far from Astugi to Eielson AFB, Alaska. Two flights in June 1957 (6002 and 6005), with another on 16 September (6008), targeted Klyuchi on Kamchatka. On the remote edge of the Soviet Union, it was a desolate area, empty of people and infrastructure, more than

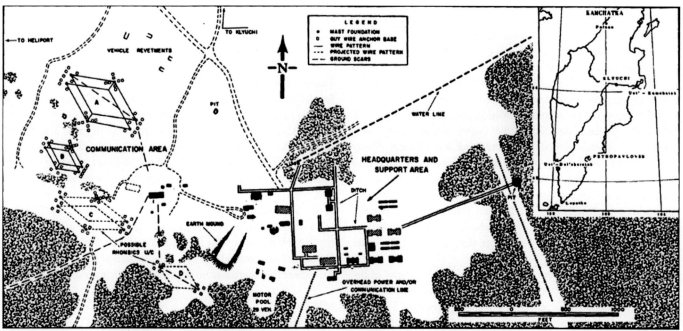

From the U-2 imagery scaled drawings were made of targets. This shows the main features of an HQ and Communications area under construction at the Klyuchi range area in 1957. (NPIC, Years of Project HTAUTOMAT, p.668)

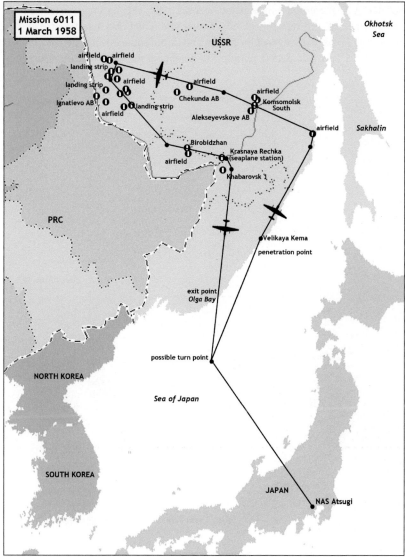

A precise route for Mission 6011 is not available as the aircraft's tracker camera failed. This one was constructed from many of the detailed target locations on the mission. Flown by 'Dirty Bird' Art 378, the aircraft was identified by Soviet radar and even experienced a flameout on the final part of the return leg. (Map by Tom Cooper based on Data SIO, NOAA, USN, NGA, GEBCO and Landsat)

1,450nm from Vladivostock, and 3,240nm and nine time zones ahead of Moscow. It was a soft overflight target. Uncertain of its possible use, Klyuchi had been identified by the Committee on Overhead Reconnaissance (COMOR) chairman James Reber in May 1957, as a likely launch or target range area for guided missiles.[4] These two U-2 flights revealed early construction work, identifying grass airfields, and even many of the triangulation points later used to track incoming warheads. The lack of major groundworks convinced analysts, as early as August 1957, that Klyuchi was almost certainly a terminal range area rather than a launch site. By November firm connections were being drawn between Tyuratam as the ICBM launch site and Klyuchi as the target range.[5] Later flights, other sources and satellite imagery tracked progress on Klyuchi. These strategic U-2 missions ultimately paved the way for the major Cobra Ball and Cobra Dane programmes that collected Soviet test ICBM telemetry for the rest of the Cold War.

The detachment's first major penetration of Soviet airspace from Astugi was also the last. On 1 March 1958, Mission 6011 used 'Dirty Bird' Art 378, flown by Tom Crull. Early flight planning suggested using a point of entry (PoE) into the Soviet target area from China, or possibly North Korea, to disguise the U-2's departure base. However, at some stage, that idea was rejected and to avoid overflying a third country the PoE was later switched to the Soviet coast itself. Image frame numbering suggests it first headed towards Sovetskaya Gavan, then tracked broadly westwards to take in the primary target, the Ukrainia (Seyshevo) bomber base in the Amur Oblast, with its Badger and Bison bombers. It then headed back out to the coast and kept clear of PRC airspace. On this flight, the usually reliable tracker camera failed. This was later attributed to a new procedure that told pilots to turn that camera on 30 minutes after take-off, instead of just after take-off. By 30 minutes, now at high altitude, the tracker film had frozen and so the camera failed. Without that precise data, and in the absence of any other declassified information to precisely plot its route, much of its flight path is estimated.

Fortunately, the main A2 camera performed well and generated a wealth of high-quality imagery. As Crull withdrew from the target area he experienced a flameout, attributed to very severe turbulence, but safely recovered to Astugi. The mission provoked a strong Soviet protest, that precisely detailed the flight's PoE and exit points with times. It demonstrated that the 'Dirty Bird' concealment efforts were far from successful. An internal CIA report the following month suggested that: 'With increased numbers and types of Russian radars, as well as the obvious increase in efficiency of their operations, it is Operations' opinion that no matter how Mission 6011 had been planned, it would have been detected and tracked…'[6] It caused Eisenhower to impose another immediate ban on Soviet overflights.[7]

Unable to mount further overflights of the USSR because of the protests, Det C was soon looking for alternative missions. The first was over Indonesia where rebels were resisting President Sukarno's regime. The U-2 flights became part of a wider CIA-led, covert operations package. The US Naval Air Station at Cubi Point in the Philippines was used as the staging base for these overflights. Airlifted there on 21 March 1958, missions began a week later. A series of 30 flights were mounted up to 11 June 1958, mainly flown by three aircraft (Arts 342, 353 and 358), with photo processing undertaken at nearby Clark AFB by the temporarily activated URPIC–2. Many of the planned missions were either cancelled,

curtailed, or less productive than expected, mostly due to poor weather. Although collecting useful intelligence, this was much more a 'tactical' tasking, than a strategic one.

Taiwan Straits

In 1958 tensions between the PRC and nationalist China heightened, leading to fears of a possible communist invasion of Taiwan. Det C's U-2s were called upon to collect more intelligence. Staging out of Naha Air Base, Okinawa, Mission 6012 took off for China and covered the coastal area from Fu Chou (Fuzhou), opposite Taiwan, northwards towards Shanghai. Its nine hour 20 minute flight took CIA pilot Lyle Rudd past 18 airfields, achieving high-quality imagery of 13. This was the first of five periodic flights up to 9 September 1958 when 6019 imaged from south of Taiwan, as far as Guangzhou, north of Hong Kong.[8] The final mission of the series was 6023 on 22 October. These coastal belt missions reassured the Americans and Taiwanese that there was no build-up of PRC invasion forces.[9]

Mill Town

There are two rather intriguing missions launched from Cubi Point in May 1959. Mission 6025 on 12 May 1959 and 6028 on 14 and 15 May, both described as Operation 'Mill Town'. These are briefly mentioned in Agency records with the coverage listed, rather disingenuously, as 'SW China and Tibet'. No significant data has been discovered for Mission 6025, but some misfiled details for 6028 provide details pointing to a support mission for CIA insurgency

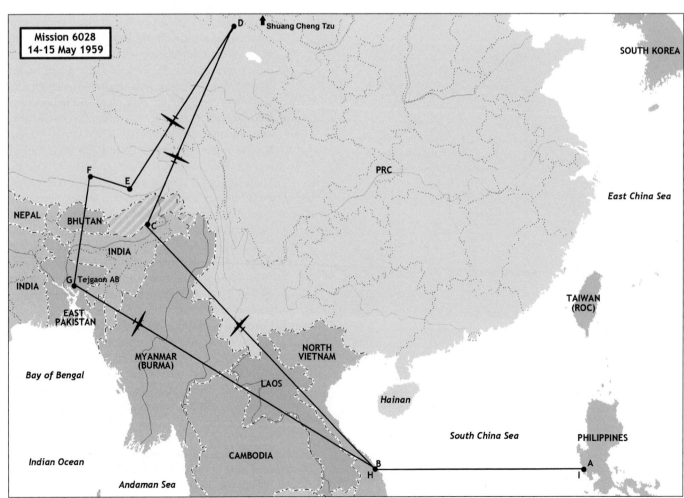

The two 'Mill Town' missions were very long-range flights, that searched close to Koko Nor Lake area in connection with Agency insurgency operations against the Chinese in Tibet. Mission 6028, at least required a fuel stop at Tejgaon airfield, in then then East Pakistan. (Map by Tom Cooper based on Data SIO, NOAA, USN, NGA, GEBCO and Landsat)

A shot of southern Lhasa, including part of the Kyi Chu River, probably taken in May 1959 on Mission 6025 or 6028. Although not the mission's primary target, US analysts were interested in signs of Chinese military activity in and around the city. (CIA)

operations, close to Koko Nor Lake in Tibet, directed against the Chinese.

Having departed Cubi Point, Lyle Rudd flew west, making landfall at Da Nang in Vietnam. He headed north-west, until crossing the River Bramaphutra and turning north-north-east, on a 700nm leg towards the Gobi Desert in China. Rudd turned back close to the River Heihe, just within photographic range of Koko Nor Lake. The Koko Nor area became a priority target for two reasons. First, the CIA was then working with Tibetan guerrillas, to train and equip them to disrupt the Chinese road network in the area, the only real land connection to China. U-2 mission imagery probably helped find local Chinese forces, create accurate maps of the area and identify possible landing grounds for Agency operated C-130s, to insert guerrillas into the area.[10] Second, the area on the eastern side of Koko Nor became important for the PRC's nuclear weapon research and manufacture programme. Roughly 500 miles west of that, on the edge of the Taklamakan desert and adjoining the Gobi Desert, was the Lop Nor nuclear test site. When Rudd turned back, he was also just 150nm south of Shuang Cheng Tzu, a nuclear research/test facility, known to have opened in 1958, today known as Jiuquan. He headed back towards Lhasa in Tibet, before landing at Tejgaon airfield, an old US World War Two facility, now home of the Bangladesh Air Force museum in then East Pakistan.[11] The U-2 was expected to remain at Tejgaon for some nine to 12 hours before it headed back to Cubi Point. How long it was on the ground is unknown. Pakistan's president Ayub had approved use of the airfield on 28 April 1959.[12]

Typhoon Hunting

The U-2 was the first aircraft ever capable of flying over typhoons at a sufficient altitude to photograph whole systems. It also provided a wonderful opportunity to practice their cover as meteorological research aircraft. From Astugi AB on 14 and 15 July 1958, there

were two missions (1774 and 1775) flown in Art 359 over typhoon 'Winnie'. Their missions were coordinated by the 54th Weather Reconnaissance Squadron and the U-2 carried its A1 camera to photograph these incredible weather phenomena. There were further flights, including 1778 (Art 342), to track typhoon 'Grace' on 3 September 1958 and 1779 on 25 September 1958 tracking 'Ida'. For typhoon Ida three detachment U-2s were even briefly evacuated to Naha, on Okinawa, to avoid the storm.[13]

The Agency worked hard to promote these activities publicly, even preparing a 'publicity kit' in conjunction with the National Advisory Committee for Aeronautics.[14] In March 1959 at the American Meteorological Society annual meeting, Dr Robert Fletcher together with colleagues, showed some of the collected typhoon imagery as part of a presentation on cloud and storm formations. The following month and in later years, details and images were published in several related professional journals.[15] As well as generating cover publicity, they helped disguise a small number of HASP (High Altitude Sampling Programme) missions, largely hidden from public discussion, because of Japanese political sensitivities.

Secret Sampling

Detachment C was involved in a sequence of U-2 flights that have remained well hidden from nearly all official references. Even their mission numbers, dates and details are still absent from the mainstream public CIA archive. However, it was possible to pull together some fragmentary details. These occasional flights took place between October 1958 and March 1960 over Japan, numbered in the same sequence as those from Cubi Point over Indonesia, from March 1957.

Searching through records, the breakthrough came with the discovery of a full flight route planned for the last of these, Mission 1787, flown on 24 February 1960.[16] This small number of flights

Table 1: Fallout Sampling Missions 1780–1787		
Mission	Date	Details
1780	11 Oct 1958	
1781	6 Nov 1958	Art 353, take-off 1914Z, landed 0315Z
1782	7 Nov 1958	
1783	7 Nov 1958	Art 353, take-off 2059Z, landed 0520Z. Entry point one hour after take-off
1784	8 Nov 1958	Mission cancelled. Ground abort, radio failure
1785	29 Mar 1959	
1786	21 Feb 1960	Art 353, take-off 2330Z, landed 0740Z
1787	24 Feb 1960	Art 353, take-off 1400Z, landed 2200Z

(CIA Mission Documents)

were Agency mounted covert nuclear fallout sampling missions. They followed very closely prescribed flight parameters, particularly in terms of speed and altitude. Art 353, configured with a hatch sampler, was to depart Astugi and head north, entering a tightly specified flight pattern. As the mission progressed and fuel was burned off, it climbed higher. By Point D, it was at 65,250ft; Point F, 66,000ft; Point L, 68,500ft and Point R, 70,000ft. The sampling filters were turned on and off at prearranged times. During these missions, the U-2 had to fly within a specific speed range, related to its altitude (121kts for 65,000ft, 108kts for 70,000ft) and had to take account of the outside air temperature. All of this was necessary to ensure reasonably consistent air flows through the filter papers, to allow comparable data measurements to be made.[17]

The 'F-2 Foil' equipment, required a special hatch installation, mounted on the lower opening of the Q-bay. Samples were collected on a series of just six 16-inch diameter filter papers, which were rotated into and out of the sampling position. When a filter was

in place, its exposure to the airflow was controlled by a door in the air inlet duct. This was opened by an electric actuator, allowing air to be ducted in, passed through the filter and passed out of the duct's rear.[18] An 'automatic observer' camera in the Q-bay, photographed a repeat of the cockpit display indicator lights, plus a duplicate altimeter reading, outside air temperature reading and clock, every 15 seconds.[19] Once a filter paper exposure was completed, the next cycled into position. The whole F-2 package weighed 171lb. This nuclear fallout collection device was different from that used in the early USAF U-2s in their High Altitude Sampling Programme with its 'hard-nosed' aircraft (see Volume 1).

1787 is the only mission in this series for which significant details have been found. For the others, it is impossible to be certain of their precise routes. Whether these missions were mounted in direct response to specific events, or as part of routine scheduling, is unknown. However, there were Soviet test explosions over western Kazakhstan, launched from Kapustin Yar, on 1 and 3 November 1958 (Joe 82 and 83) and may account for planned missions 1781–1784. Art 353 was not one of the original 'hard nose' sampling aircraft but carried the specialised HASP payload pack as required.

Fallout monitoring missions were very sensitive for the Japanese government. On 1 March 1954, the 23-man crew of the fishing boat *Lucky Dragon* had passed through the fallout cloud from the US 'Castle Bravo' nuclear test, on the Marshall Islands. All the men

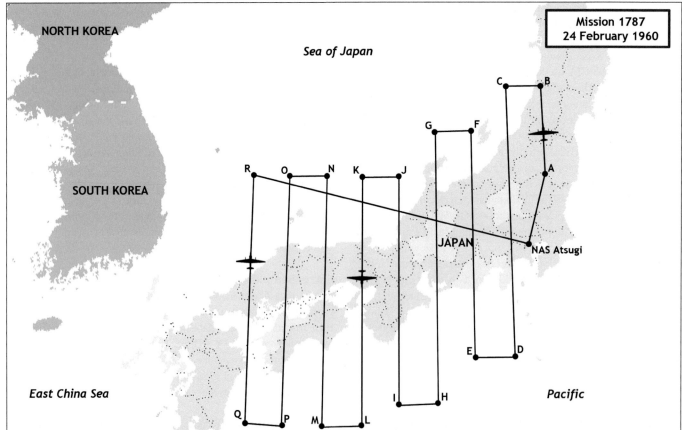

Mission 1787 was flown on 24 February 1960. A small number of fallout sampling flights were covertly flown by the CIA over Japan between 1958 and 1960. The routes had to be flown very precisely. (Map by Tom Cooper based on Data SIO, NOAA, USN, NGA, GEBCO and Landsat)

The air sampling scoop was the only section of the fallout sampling kit that was externally visible. The remainder of the equipment was mounted inside the Q-bay. (USAF)

6035 aborted partway through with an oxygen system failure. Mission 6037, on 3 September, covered Tibet on its outbound route. 6038 and 6042 (4 and 9 September) used identical routes into northern China, on the edge of the Gobi Desert and within 150 miles of the Mongolian border, searching for indications of the Chinese nuclear programme. Flown by Art 353 that operation was far from successful. There were failures of its System III and System VI, plus problems with the B camera, most likely caused by incorrectly set mechanical camera programmer equipment. 6040 was flown on 7 September over Laos, but abandoned due to worse than forecast weather. 6044 mounted over Tibet on 12 September, was the final mission before heading home.

suffered acute radiation sickness and one soon died. The event caused immediate panic across Japan, the public concerned about the safety of tuna fish for human consumption. It sparked a strong anti-nuclear movement. The US probably feared public revelation of the fallout monitoring flights might provoke further panic and increase anti-American sentiment.

Growing Commitments

The photographic deployments continued. A group of missions code-named 'South Gate' were mounted from August 1959. 6035 launched from Naha on 29 August and landed at Takhli in Thailand. This rather neglected Thai airbase, soon became an important staging and recovery base for U-2 missions until Agency operations in the region ended. Having covered parts of Laos and Vietnam, Mission

Mission 6045 was a single flight, over the Kuril Islands from Japan on 1 November 1959, flown in Art 353 by Buster Edens. Two days later, the same aircraft was back in Thailand. 'Quick Kick', Mission 6046, was another staging operation, where Art 353 went far into China and Tibet, piloted by Bill McMurry. Operation 'Topper', was Det C's final return to Takhli for three further missions covering Tibet and China. This comprised a pair of flights (6049 and 6050) on 30 March, and 6054, the Koko Nor mission flight, on 5 April 1959, flown by McMurry in Art 349. His otherwise successful flight ended ignominiously when he ran out of fuel just short of Takhli and force

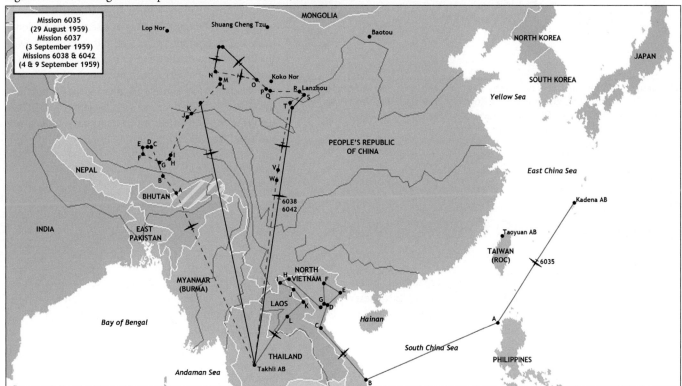

A series of flights, mainly aimed at the PRC, in autumn 1959, began with deployment from Naha AB on Okinawa to Takhli in Thailand (6035), flying a complex route over Vietnam and Laos first. (Map by Tom Cooper based on Data SIO, NOAA, USN, NGA, GEBCO and Landsat)

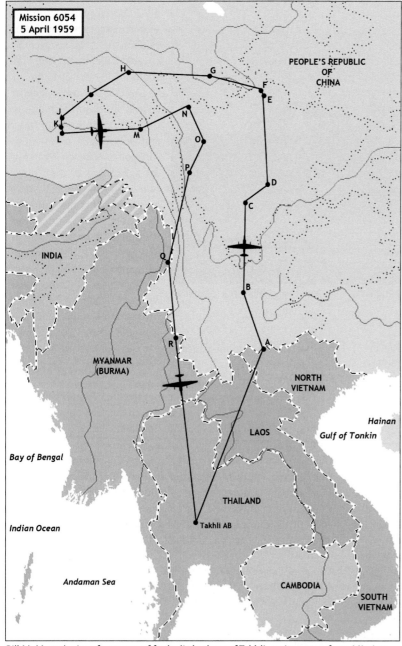

**Mission 6054
5 April 1959**

Bill McMurry's aircraft ran out of fuel a little short of Takhli, on its return from Mission 6054, to the far north of China to cover the Koko Nor area. Disassembled, it was flown to the US for repair. (Map by Tom Cooper based on Data SIO, NOAA, USN, NGA, GEBCO and Landsat)

landed. Nine days later his aircraft was recovered to the airfield and spirited away in a C-124, repaired and later returned to service.[20]

Det C's basing had always proved problematic. Pushed out of Watertown before a permanent location was identified, it was resented by US forces in Japan – especially the USAF, intent on building its high altitude reconnaissance capability with its RB-57s. That was compounded by the Japanese government's discomfort at having U-2s present on its soil. This was especially apparent after Mission 6011 drew voluble public Soviet protests, plus the well-publicised forced landing on 24 September 1959. Returning from a typhoon monitoring mission Tom Crull in Art 360, had run out of fuel and force landed at Fukisawa Airport, close to Astugi. The aircraft was soon surrounded by curious Japanese onlookers. An anxious CIA security team, all in civilian clothes, arrived and, in attempting to protect the aircraft, created even more interest by brandishing pistols. Lots of photographs made it into the local press.[21] It was the same Article that would be flown by Gary Powers when he was shot down on 1 May 1960.

The final straw was Gary Power's loss. Following that, many public demonstrations pushed the Japanese government to request the U-2's withdrawal from its territory by 8 July 1960. With nowhere else in-theatre to go and only two airframes on strength, the detachment was wound-up. Aircraft and pilots were transferred back to Edwards AFB.[22] Unsurprisingly, operations in Asia became even more sensitive. Potential hosts became even more cautious in granting permission, even for short periods of operations, for fear of the political fallout.

Operational Capability

In the aftermath of the Powers shoot-down, operational basing was rethought. Finding overseas hosts for long-term U-2 operations became all but impossible. Even the British, who still had a stake in U-2 operations, were dead set against a permanent presence in the UK, or at its overseas bases, concerned about negative publicity associated with the U-2. Likewise, the Japanese. The best the Agency could hope for was temporary deployment facilities. The one exception was Taiwan.

2

BLACK CATS AND CHURCH DOOR

The CIA already had an extensive intelligence relationship with the nationalist Chinese well before the U-2. Agency and Taiwanese crews had for several years been flying night missions inserting agents, leaflet dropping and conducting electronic intelligence (ELINT) missions over areas of China adjacent to Taiwan. From late 1956 a few nationalist pilots were trained to fly occasional high altitude reconnaissance flights using loaned American RB-57s.[1]

In December 1958 the United States agreed to provide U-2s to the Nationalist Air Force, via the CIA. President Eisenhower

and the State Department gave formal approval for a Taiwanese detachment in August 1960, the main details soon agreed with the Government of the Republic of China (GRC). Although a joint operation, as with the British, the Americans had the final say over important details. A July 1960 CIA paper proposed supplying two aircraft in Taiwanese markings using the assigned cryptonym 'TACKLE'. They would fly the length and breadth of Asia from 1962 to 1974.[2] Attempting to disguise their involvement, the Agency used convoluted arrangements to transfer the airframes to Taiwan.

Lockheed provided repair estimates for two 'damaged' U-2s at the deliberately inflated cost of $800,000. The high estimate was rejected by the Agency, so the airframes were offered outright to Lockheed for 'salvage' at $250,000 each. Rebuilt and modified by Lockheed they were quietly sold to Taiwan at $1.2 million each (Art 358 and 378) with the selected pilots trained in the US at Del Rio. Fully 'repaired' the U-2s were despatched to Taoyuan airfield accompanied by USAF personnel assigned to the 6213th Support Squadron Mobile Training Team and CIA staff undercover as Lockheed personnel.[3] They arrived in Taiwan in January 1961 and missions were assigned the code name CHURCH DOOR.

The CIA's rationale for agreeing to an arrangement with nationalist China and using ROC pilots is not difficult to understand. Flights over the PRC would fill a black hole in America's intelligence picture and comprised two major elements. First, the US's highest priority was to collect intelligence on the PRC's nascent nuclear programme. Second, were missions of more immediate importance to the Taiwanese. These meant keeping a close watch on the possibility of PRC invasion and constructing a detailed Order of Battle (ORBAT) of forces opposite Taiwan on the Chinese mainland. These became of less interest to the Americans once original fears of communist invasion declined.

Using nationalist crews to undertake the missions removed risk to Agency pilots and gave a veneer of deniability. This was balanced against the risk of operations being penetrated by PRC agents and fears of pilot defection, either on ideological grounds or under duress. Det H, as it was known to the CIA, used specially trained pilots belonging to 35 'Black Cat' Squadron, an independent unit that reported directly to the Commander in Chief of the Republic's Air Force. These incredibly brave men flew the U-2 up to 1974 and lost 12 pilots (including two captured) in training, accidents and operational missions over the PRC.

The mission approval process adopted was a joint one, similar to the arrangement with the British. Flights were planned by the Americans and approved by the Special Group in Washington DC. Nationalist Chinese assent to missions was given on an individual basis via General Fu-en I the Black Cat's Squadron commander, by Ching-kuo Chiang, also vice-chair of the ROC's National Security Bureau.[4]

Interwoven with Det H activities were Detachment G operations based at Edwards AFB. It was responsible for U-2 related research, test and development activities. Sometimes these were for fleet-wide application and others were one-off projects installed into a single airframe. Its operational task was to provide a 'mobile capability' that could be rapidly sent anywhere in the world. Sometimes this involved deploying aircraft and/or personnel to work alongside, or supplement, Detachment H. Det G's role and missions are separately explored in Chapter 4.

Changing Dynamics

The recovery of the first successful satellite imagery in August 1960 introduced a new element to planning U-2 missions over Asia. The ground coverage capabilities of the Corona satellites were huge, but the downside was that its imagery was not initially very detailed. Large features like runways could be seen but the camera lacked the resolution quality necessary for detailed analysis which the U-2 imagery was routinely collecting. However, the two programmes did overlap. Corona imagery was often used to identify new, large, never seen before targets which could then be overflown by U-2s when possible. However, a major problem soon emerged. The loss of Yin Chin Wong in his RB-57D over Beijing in October 1959 and Gary Powers in 1960 proved the SA-2 SAM was a real threat. Early Corona imagery often did not always allow identification of new SA-2 installations or provide adequate detail of existing sites to assess if they were operational. For U-2s to identify SA-2

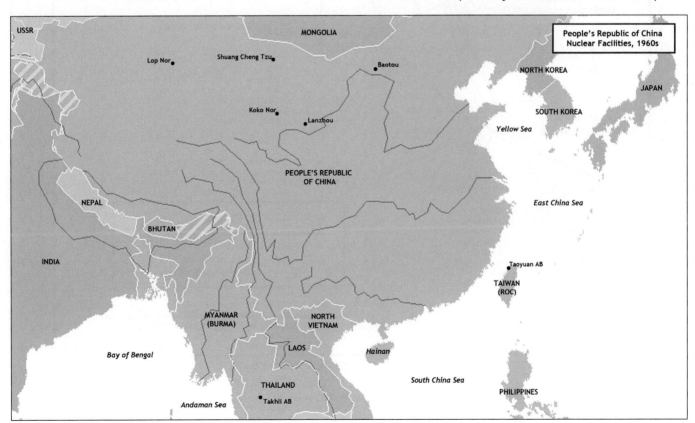

The five main Chinese nuclear-related sites targeted by U-2 overflights in the 1960s. Lanzhou was the closest, still over 1,200nm from both Taoyuan and Takhli in a straight line. (Map by Tom Cooper based on Data SIO, NOAA, USN, NGA, GEBCO and Landsat/Copernicus)

GRC100 13 JANUARY 1962

GRC100 was the first mission launched by the nationalist pilots, far to the north, aimed at the Shuang Cheng Tzu facility. It was from there that in 1966 the Chinese launched their first successful nuclear missile test aimed at the Lop Nor test ground.

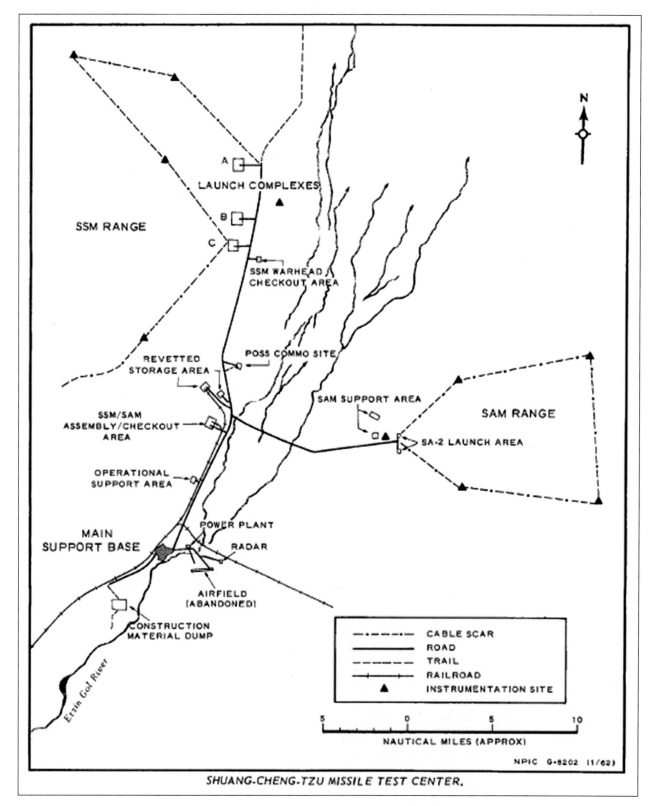

SHUANG-CHENG-TZU MISSILE TEST CENTER.

Line drawing of the Shuang Cheng Tzu, extracted from the imagery collected by GRC100. (CIA)

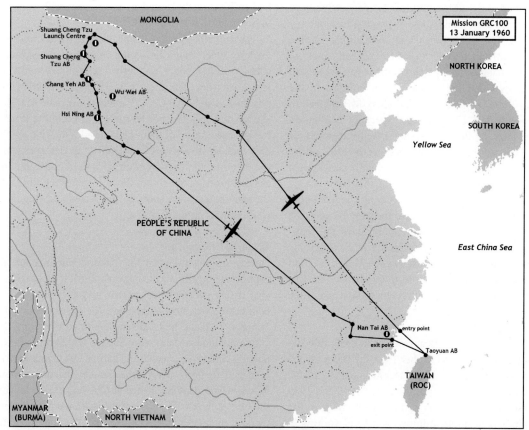

The great distances involved meant the route for GRC100 had to be direct, with no feints or additional targets. (Map by Tom Cooper based on Data SIO, NOAA, USN, NGA, GEBCO, Landsat/Copernicus and SK Telecom)

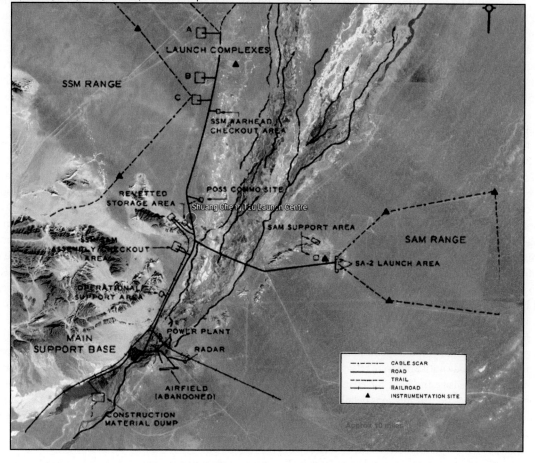

When the 1960 scale line drawing is overlaid onto modern satellite imagery the extent to which they compare so closely is remarkable. It says a great deal about the skills of the PIs and CIA/NPIC graphic artists of the day. (CIA, Data SIO, NOAA, USN, NGA, GEBCO, Landsat/Copernicus, SK Telecom)

emplacements, they had to fly sufficiently close to adequately image them but remain outside their lethal range or manage to avoid any missiles fired at them. The gap between U-2 and Corona satellite imaging capabilities contributed to the loss of aircraft and crews. As the quality of satellite imagery rapidly improved, the gap decreased.

It has been suggested that the regular U-2 overflights of the PRC, together with the CIA's low-level STBARNUM penetration missions, using modified B-17s and later specially configured RB-69s, actually assisted the PRC to develop a well-integrated air defence system.[5] To counter high altitude missions the PRC, rather than just relying on fixed sites as the Soviets did, quietly used at least some of its SA-2s as semi-mobile systems, moving them to locations where U-2s were known to overfly. In constructing the fixed sites they effectively funnelled U-2 overflights into the gaps between the fixed sites, where they had sometimes quietly deployed the semi-mobile units. These were kept 'hidden' from the U-2's electronic sensors, not being turned on until the last possible moment. Then they rapidly acquired and fired at the close-to-overhead U-2. This significantly increased their chances of a direct hit or fatal near miss.

Hunting the PRC's Nuclear Programme

Secretly China had begun its early nuclear research in 1955, aided by Soviet scientists for a short while. In October 1957, the USSR agreed to supply a 'sample of an atomic bomb' and technical data to enable Beijing to manufacture a nuclear weapon. Between 1955 and 1959 roughly 250 Chinese nuclear scientists and engineers went to the Soviet Union to train, with a similar number of experts working in the PRC to help develop the nuclear industry. However, during 1959 as the Sino-Soviet relationship fell apart the USSR discontinued all assistance to the PRC.[6]

During that early period, several key locations were selected for nuclear research and construction work began. Two of the most important became the Baotou uranium enrichment facility and the Lanzhou gaseous diffusion plant, that enriched uranium, where work began in 1958. Lop Nor, a remote location in northern China, was selected as its principal nuclear test ground in late 1958 with Koko Nor a major research and component test centre. Shuang Cheng Tzu (now the Jiuquan satellite launch centre) became what was perhaps the PRC's largest nuclear-related complex. As well as being a missile test and space launch centre for which it is today best known, Jeffrey Richelson has described it as an early nuclear processing and component production plant too.[7] These five locations, all in northern China, were about as far as it was possible to be from prying US reconnaissance aircraft. Even after the early Detachment C missions against them, they remained high priority targets for a significant number of U-2 missions until 1968 and the cessation of deep penetration overflights. Ultimately missions to the Lanzhou and Baotou enrichment plants resulted in at least two U-2s lost, one in 1963, nearly another in late 1964 and the second in early 1965, all to SA-2s. Fortunately, the pilots of the two shot-down aircraft survived, although they would spend 19 and 17 years respectively in communist custody until both were released in 1982.

Table 2 shows just how extensive the hunt for elements of the Chinese nuclear programme became. The missions detailed indicate just overflights where the major nuclear centres appear obvious key targets. They began with American piloted Det C missions from Cubi Point in the Philippines and later Takhli. After Detachment H came into operation the pilots were Taiwanese. Det H launched their missions against the PRC's main nuclear establishments from Taoyuan, Takhli and Kunsan in South Korea. These missions were close to the limits of the U-2's operational range. It meant that flights

had to be directly routed in most cases with major feints nearly impossible.

Provision for carrying drop tanks was made on a few aircraft from 1965 to 1966. They carried the same amount of fuel (1,316lb/200 gallons) as the more regularly used slipper tanks and could be jettisoned from their underwing pylons, outboard of the slipper tank positions. The USAF U-2C/F manual indicated that 'drop tanks and slipper tanks should not be carried at the same time'. No mention has yet been found of them being used operationally. Therefore, the only real way to try and fool Chinese air defences was by changing the departure and recovery airfields used and sometimes reversing the directions of the routes flown. Attempting to repeatedly overfly the same targets in a short period risked allowing the PRC time to reposition its air defence assets.

Shuang Cheng Tzu

Having trained pilots in the US and put in place the necessary support arrangements during early 1961, it was to be nearly a whole year before overflight operations began. Back in the US, the 5412 Committee was slow to approve the first missions. Finally, on 13 January 1962, the first Taiwanese piloted overflight flew far across China piloted by Major Huai Shen Chen. Mission GRC100 targeted Shuang Cheng Tzu, which the earlier Det C missions had not quite managed to find.[8] Before the launch, the detachment received a message from Colonel Beerli at CIA HQ: 'Wish all your personnel the best of luck with HQs appreciation for your patience and hard work in maintaining this capability.'[9] Although no detailed route is yet publicly available, details of the airfields imaged in GRC100's Initial Photographic Interpretation Report (IPIR) indicates the essential very direct route. Using a B camera, oblique imagery of the Shuang Cheng Tzu site appears in the IPIR, with buildings, roads and tracks readily identifiable, although the images are not good enough for reproduction here.[10] However, the report and images identify the launch complexes, SAM site and support facilities with certainty.[11] It also overflew Lanzhou but cloud made detailed analysis impossible. Major Chen's flight was detected by PRC radar but their fighters were unable to reach him. His flight lasted eight hours 40 minutes and on his return, he was taken to the unit's hangar to be congratulated by Chiang Kai-shek himself and the CIA Chief of Station. He was awarded a nationalist decoration, and presented with a wristwatch and envelope of money, as was customary on such auspicious occasions.[12]

Imagery from this first CHURCH DOOR mission was quickly transported by C-118 to the 67th Reconnaissance Technical Squadron at Yakota AB in Japan for full processing and exploitation. Colonel Roy Stanley worked on the imagery from GRC100. As he has explained the early Taiwanese flown missions were very long ones and 'they kept on coming, month after month for the next nearly nine years'.[13]

These missions also carried SIGINT Systems III and VI, in addition to their camera fit. Taiwanese U-2 pilot General Mike Hua has explained that PRC radar coverage of the mainland was good. Although the U-2s were radio silent, the passing of communications between PRC air defence units allowed Taiwanese Communications Intelligence (COMINT) operators, at their ground listening stations, to follow their progress.[14]

Confidence grew within the detachment as it mounted some more conventional and successful missions monitoring the communist Chinese military build-up along the Taiwan Straits in June–July 1962.

The Secrets of Koko Nor

Det C missions 6025 and 6028 from May 1959 had flown close to the large Koko Nor (Qinghai) lake in the hunt for the Shuang Cheng Tzu and other potential nuclear facilities. Mission GRC102, flown on 23 February 1962 by 'Gimo' Yang was another marathon overflight. This time it specifically targeted Koko Nor. His point of entry was over Shanghai, heading generally north-west passing via Sian (Xi'an) and Lanzhou up to the eastern edge of Koko Nor, where he reversed course and headed back towards Taiwan. He exited near Fuzhou. Around the eastern side of Koko Nor, there were numerous test trenches, suspected mining activity and related extraction work. To the east of the lake, there were signs of more mining activity and on the lakeshore indications of mineral processing. Within a few years, there was related railway construction and the area became better known as the Haiyan complex (also referred to as the 'Ninth Academy' or 'Factory 221'). A major nuclear weapons research and development centre, it was designed around the Soviet Arzamas-16 (Sarov) closed city model. It included facilities for high explosive and fissile component production and final weapons assembly and was active into the 1980s.[15] It was at Factory 221 that the PRC's first 16 nuclear test weapons were assembled and transported to the Lop Nor proving ground. Likened to the US Los Alamos facility, part of it is now a tourist attraction with decommissioned buildings and a museum.[16]

GRC113 on 19 June 1962 targeted the Shuang Cheng Tzu missile centre again. Flown by Tiger Wang it followed a very similar route to the very first mission, GRC100. Having flown close up to the Mongolian border Wang headed southwards. He passed over the range from the north and activated his B camera for the first time.

Technical Problems

Taiwanese missions were affected by several factors that contributed to serious losses over time. Flameouts plagued the U-2's engine, sometimes with fatal consequences. If the engine failed at high altitude it could not successfully be restarted until the U-2 had descended to around 35,000ft which then left them prey to PRC fighter aircraft. There were early concerns that the flameouts were caused by contaminated fuel or even sabotage.[17] Their main cause took some time to establish.

Mike Hua has explained that it was not until June 1964 that the flameout problem was properly resolved. A Lockheed test pilot visited Taiwan and used a Det G aircraft with an instrumented engine. He discovered that the air temperature gradient around Taiwan between 40,000ft and 60,000ft was different from most other parts of the world. The solution was simply the adoption of marginally higher power settings at increased altitudes which overcame the problem.[18]

Another significant issue for these U-2 pilots was that their aircraft became prone to generator failures. Without generator power, the autopilot failed. Aircraft then had to be flown manually, always tricky for any length of time at high altitude. Pilots needed to work hard to avoid stalling their aircraft whilst at the same time avoid it passing its 'never exceed' speed that could lead to in-flight disintegration. The cameras would not work without electrical power, nor the SIGINT systems. There was only an emergency battery to power the most essential systems to get them home.

The continuing generator failures soon appeared in the Det H monthly commanders' reports in April 1962. Art 352 experienced three generator failures in quick succession. These were attributed to wires breaking loose, as the harnesses and terminals that held them became brittle and fractured after repeated high altitude exposure to extreme sub-zero temperatures. For Art 358 examination revealed that the generator's bearings were burned out and 'ground to small particles'. Even as a replacement aircraft (Art 378) arrived on 31 March 1962 ferried across the Pacific, the pilot reported he had lost generator power too.[19] These problems were only resolved after a stand-down on 28 February 1963 where the fault was finally attributed to poor quality control during manufacture of the generator bearings.[20]

Mike Hua departed Taoyuan on 11 August 1962 (GRC125) for an overflight mission. Partway through he experienced generator failure and decided to abandon the flight. His situation was further complicated because he was over 1,200 miles and three hours' flying time from home. Heading home with a continuous undercast beneath him meant finding Taoyuan was very difficult. He was only able to do so when a brief break in the cloud layer enabled him to

Table 2: The U-2 hunt for the Chinese nuclear programme			
Mission	Date	Pilot	Targets and notes
6025	12 May 1959	Crull	Koko Nor, Shuang Cheng Tzu close to Lop Nor
6028	14 May 1959	Rudd	Koko Nor, Shuang Cheng Tzu, close to Lop Nor
6037	3 Sep 1959	McMurry	Koko Nor, Lanzhou
6038	4 Sep 1959	Crull	Koko Nor, Lanzhou, close to Shuang Cheng Tzu
6042	9 Sep 1959	Crull	Koko Nor, Lanzhou, close to Shuang Cheng Tzu
6054	5 Apr 1960	McMurry	Koko Nor, Lanzhou
GRC100	12 Jan 1962	Chen	Shuang Cheng Tzu, near Lanzhou and Koko Nor
GRC102	23 Feb 1962	Gimo Yang	Lanzhou
GRC113	19 Jun 1962	Wang	Shuang Cheng Tzu
GRC144	28 Mar 1963	Wang	Shuang Cheng Tzu, Lanzhou and Baotou areas
GRC153	3 Jun 1963	Mike Hua	Lanzhou
GRC156	12 Jun 1963	Mike Hua	Baotou, Xi'an
GRC176	25 Sep 1963	Lee	Shuang Cheng Tzu
GRC178	26 Sep 1963	Robin Yeh	Baotou
GRC184	1 Nov 1963	Robin Yeh	Shuang Cheng Tzu. Lost to SA-2, captured
C224C	31 Oct 1964	Chang	Lanzhou
C284C	22 Nov 1964	Chang	Lanzhou. Mission aborted
C304C	25 Nov 1964	Johnny Yang	Lanzhou. Mission aborted
C344C	19 Dec 1964		Lanzhou. Mission aborted
C015C	8 Jan 1965	Johnny Yang	Lanzhou
C025C	10 Jan 1965	Chang	Baotou. Lost to SA-2, captured

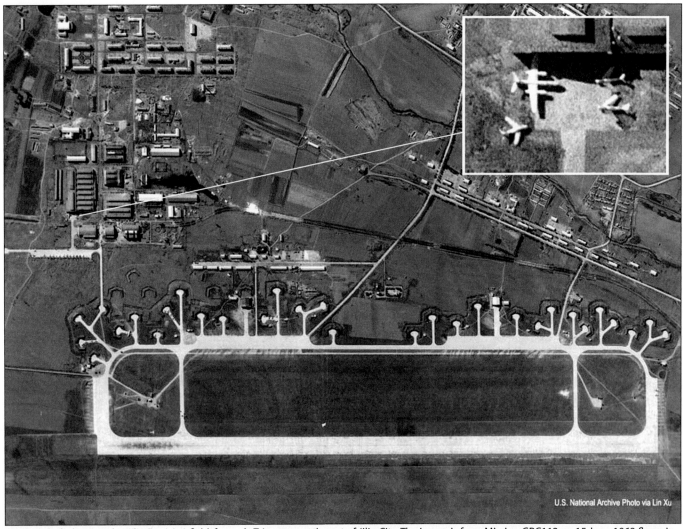

U.S. National Archive Photo via Lin Xu

Overhead of what is today Jilin Ertaizi airfield, formerly Tsingtau, north-east of Jilin City. The image is from Mission GRC112 on 15 June 1962 flown in Art 378 by Gimo Yang. The buildings to the top left of the image indicate a military repair and/or maintenance depot. (NARA, Lin Xu via Chris Pocock)

identify the Tachen Islands and set a correct course for home. He recalled being 'exhausted' when he finally got out of the cockpit.[21]

On 8 September 1962 (GRC127) ROC pilot Huai Chen was shot down in Art 378 (one of the early 'Dirty Bird' conversions reconfigured back to a U-2C) by an SA-2, although nothing was known of it until the loss was announced by PRC radio. In response the Taiwanese government publicly admitted its operation of the U-2.[22] A reflective internal memo to the CIA's James Cunningham a few days later not only bemoaned Chen's loss, but that there was no information available about how it had occurred. He hinted at the need for equipment to report the U-2's progress during missions, which emerged as the 'Birdwatcher' system in 1963–1964.[23]

Evolving Defences

As if the aircraft's mechanical problems were not serious enough, PRC air defence forces implemented increasingly effective tactics. MiGs always pursued U-2 intrusions. Unable to reach them, they circled below and awaited a technical issue forcing the U-2 to descend within their grasp. SA-2 sites began to rapidly appear. Mike Hua even imaged some empty SA-2 sites on the edge of Peking. Unknown to the nationalist Chinese, the normally resident missiles had been deployed to alternative locations where commanders believed the U-2s would overfly.[24]

Not known in the west at the time, Chinese SA-2 use faced another major limitation. The PRC's deep ideological and material split with Moscow by 1960 meant no new Soviet military equipment

was available to them. Previously supplied with five SA-2 batteries and 62 missiles, until the Chinese could succeed in reverse engineering them and construct new equipment, their supply of SA-2s was strictly limited. It provides an additional explanation why PRC forces moved around some of their SA-2s and developed tactics to improve their lethality. From 1962 the U-2's System XII, an early SA-2 launch detector, at least gave pilots a cockpit indication and an audible headphone warning.

Photo Processing

The processing and interpretation arrangements for most U-2 imagery are covered in Volume 1. However, processing imagery from U-2 missions over Asia posed significant challenges because of the much greater distances involved in crossing the Pacific to reach the north-eastern continental United States. There were essentially two options. Do the work in the Pacific theatre, or transport it to the US for processing.

Much of the exposed film was airlifted directly to the US to Eastman Kodak's 'Bridgehead' facility in Rochester, NY or the US Air Force Special Projects Production Facility (AFSPPF) in Building P–1900 at Westover AFB, Massachusetts.[25] The processed film was taken by courier to the National Photographic Intelligence Centre (NPIC) in Washington DC and transported on to other customers. The workloads at Bridgehead and the AFSPPF were in a constant state of flux as the intensity of missions and the amount of film they generated fluctuated. This was particularly so once satellite imagery started to be processed from August 1960. The arrival of bulk loads of film for processing at one location would see work diverted to the other. Backlogs would build if a deployed operation generated large amounts of photographic material from several missions and it was shipped back to the US as a single load. Early on, materials were often transported by C-47s and C-54s, later Military Airlift Command C-130s and sometimes even standard civil airliners accompanied by couriers.

Yakota Air Base

The huge distances involved and the sometimes more 'tactical' nature of U-2 operations meant there was sufficient work to justify a Pacific based permanent processing facility. The 67th Tactical Reconnaissance Wing moved to Yakota AB in Japan during 1957 and absorbed personnel from the existing 548th Reconnaissance Technical Squadron. It had responsibility for processing imagery from some of the special project high altitude RB-57 reconnaissance missions launched from Japan and Taiwan.

Re-designated as the 67th RTS the facility became much more important once Taiwanese CHURCH DOOR U-2 operations began in 1962. There 67th RTS personnel worked closely alongside CIA representatives who would arrive for Temporary Duty (TDY) periods to oversee the take from individual or series of missions. Early on, the films were couriered to Yakota by air from Taoyuan where they were processed by the Air Force personnel under the eye of the CIA representative. He prepared the Initial Photographic Interpretation Report (IPIR) which was circulated before the material was forwarded to the US.[26]

Normally the 67th RTS Photographic Interpreters (PIs) worked on locally produced materials from Air Force photo-reconnaissance units. There were some very experienced 67th RTS PIs who held the highest security clearances to manage CHURCH DOOR materials. When the CIA representative arrived to deal with a mission take, the specially cleared 67th RTS personnel would be temporarily placed under his control.[27]

At Yakota this special clearance work took place behind the 'Green Door' kept under guard and entered via a cypher lock to which very few people had entry rights. To qualify for this small group of 'Top Secret Talent' cleared airmen, individuals were subjected to enhanced background checks of their families and circumstances. The unit also had some specialist machinery supplied by Eastman Kodak necessary to do their work. Once all the work was completed and the CIA staff had departed the laboratory, the space they used for the CHURCH DOOR mission processing would revert to normal 67th RTS intelligence tasks. As these missions intensified it sometimes caused significant backlogs of lower priority materials. For individual missions, squadron members worked in four shift cycles, around the clock, until the task was completed. So intense did U-2 related work become, that a one-day record was established in January 1962, when the processing laboratory developed 34,000ft of photographic materials plus 351,353ft of duplicate film and prints.[28]

As well as the main Yakota facilities sometimes a temporary lab, processing and interpretation arrangements were activated. In Asia this was known as (URPIC–Y) with Yakota personnel sometimes temporarily deployed to Clark AFB, in the Philippines, to manage U-2 mission imagery mounted from Cubi Point, over Indonesia in 1958 and for some Det C missions from Astugi. This small sub-unit was also sometimes referred to as 'URPIC-2'. It processed the imagery and undertook the initial analysis before sending it on to Yakota.

Not much is publicly known about the processing facility established in Taiwan. Among other tasks it processed the U-2's tracker camera film, making a copy before forwarding the original negatives on to the US. The work was done by nationalist Chinese staff, supplemented by representatives from the CIA and Eastman Kodak. How sophisticated the equipment they used compared to Bridgehead or the AFSPPF is unclear, but the simple fact that Eastman Kodak personnel worked there indicated that some importance was attached to their work. It seems very likely, though unconfirmed, that they did at least some of the more advanced processing work and certainly completed IPIRs for some major missions.

Well trained PIs are very good at identifying military equipment and buildings, particularly from odd angles and slightly 'fuzzy' imagery. They had to be proficient at identifying potential subjects of interest, the uses of individual industrial sites, civil and military infrastructure, town and city layouts, essentially any object that could be seen from above. It required accumulated knowledge and experience. From the early days of CHURCH DOOR operations, PIs had to learn about the everyday features of normal Chinese life and buildings in cities and towns. Even communist party journals like *China Pictorial*, were useful to PIs familiarising themselves with the terrain and infrastructure they were looking at.[29]

Watching North Korea

Operational TACKLE missions were resumed on 5 December 1962 with GRC128 over North Korea from Taoyuan flown by Mike Hua.[30] Taking in targets north of the Korean DMZ, he collected a swathe of high-quality imagery said by the Agency to be 'excellent and the pilot commended for an outstanding job. We tend to expect excellent results as a matter of course, but this mission is unique enough to merit special commendation'.[31] U-2 flights over portions of North Korea were sometimes part of missions primarily aimed at mainland China. U-2 overflights specifically aimed at North Korea were relatively infrequent. Another was flown the following year on 9 May 1963 by Taiyu 'Tiger' Wang that targeted the Liaotung peninsula, to the north-west of the DPRK's border with the PRC.

A pair of missions took place on 6 and 8 October 1963. GRC181 on 6 October was flown by Taiyu Wang followed two days later by GRC182 piloted by Lieutenant Colonel Nanping 'Terry' Lee. The first was one of the few missions aimed specifically against the DPRK. Taiyu Wang departed Taoyuan shortly after 0700 hours local time flying across the Pacific before he turned north as he approached Okinawa. He passed up the east coast of South Korea, over the Yellow Sea, before he changed course and headed over the city of Pohang, still skirting the coastline. Wang crossed the DPRK border at 0805 hours, flicked the switch that turned his B camera on to Mode 1 and did a 90-degrees left turn, broadly following the line of demarcation between the two Korean states. At the same time, he also carried System III/IV, a System IX deception jammer and System XII to indicate a SAM launch. As he reached the western coast of Korea he reversed course and headed north-east. He passed within approximately 30 miles of an SA-2 site previously identified by Mission GRC150. Wang headed back towards the east coast above the port of Tongchon. His 'Mode 1' camera operation gave horizon-to-horizon coverage and captured imagery from most of the country's inhabited areas, although he remained clear of the capital Pyongyang. Wang broadly followed the country's perimeter, before briefly covering the DPRK's interior again. Paralleling the DPRK and Chinese border he finally reached the west coast, leaving the DPRK near Ongjin at 1221 hours local time. He turned off his camera and switched over the ELINT antenna seawards and

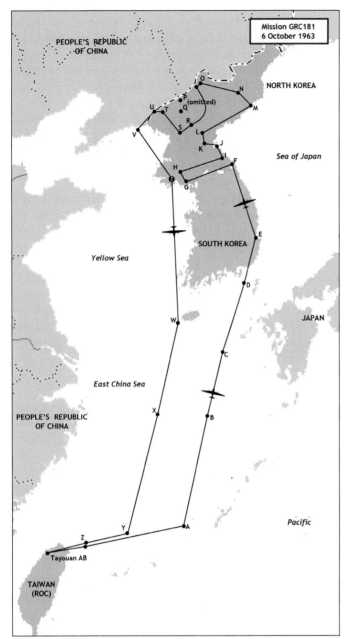

GRC181 over North Korea was flown by nationalist pilot Taiyu Wang rather than a US pilot. (Map by Tom Cooper based on Data SIO, NOAA, USN, NGA, GEBCO and Landsat/Copernicus)

headed home passing over the island of Jeje.[32] He had been over DPRK territory for three hours 16 minutes. Despite his extensive overflight, the post-flight analysis stated that 'No new significant items of intelligence were disclosed although numerous airfields and military installations were covered.'[33] The country was only imaged periodically, usually with the B camera in its least detailed sweep, mainly just for area identification purposes. Lee's 8 October route (GRC182) took him briefly through part of the DPRK passing just east of Pyongyang and then into Liaoning province of north-eastern China and across the mainland back to Taiwan.

Continued Nuclear Hunt

Mission GRC144 returned to Shuang Cheng Tzu on 28 March 1963. This time, to confuse Chinese air defences, the mission was launched from Kunsan AB in South Korea, used as a staging base. It had arrived there the previous night ferried by a US pilot. Tiger Wang was the main mission pilot with Mike Hua the reserve. Wang headed west from Kunsan and made landfall over the PRC near Qingdao. He headed far to the north-west to turn and pass over

SAAMCHAM AIRFIELD, NORTH KOREA

The DPRK was a relatively high priority for Det G/H missions but the actual coverage achieved was only sporadic, rarely meeting the official targets set. One of GRC181's targets was Saamcham airfield a fighter base in central DPRK, north of Pyongyang and relatively close to the Yŏngbyŏn nuclear reactor.

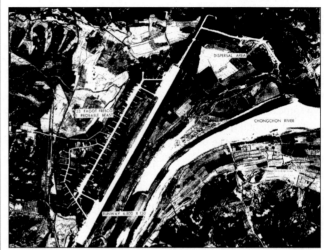

Contained in the Mission Coverage Plot is a 1963 positive image of Saamcham airfield. Not of high quality but the layout of the runway, taxiways and river Chonchong are discernible. (CIA)

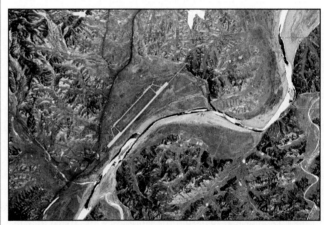

Compare that with a 1970 Corona satellite image of Saamcham. The basic layout is largely unaltered from the 1963 image and detail not incomparable. (CAST, University of Arkansas/US Geological Survey)

```
SAAMCHAM AIRFIELD  3945N 12554E
(NORTH KOREA)
7 NM NE OF SAAMCHAN AND 3.3 NM NNE OF KAECHON.
6,800 X 130 FT NE/SW CONCRETE RUNWAY, SERVICEABLE.
FACILITIES INCLUDE PARALLEL TAXIWAY WITH 2 CROSSOVER
LINKS, CONCRETE PARKING APRONS ON NE AND SW END OF
RUNWAY AND TAXIWAY, 45 REVETTED HARDSTANDS ALONG
TAXIWAY, 18 REVETTED HARDSTANDS IN DISPERSAL AREA ON
NE EDGE OF FIELD, AND A SECOND DISPERSAL AREA 3,000 FT
FROM SW END OF RUNWAY WITH ONE CONCRETE HARDSTAND AND
4 POSSIBLE UNDERGROUND STORAGE/REPAIR FACILITIES
(ENTRANCES OBSCURED BY NETTING).
DEFENSES INCLUDE FOUR 6-GUN AAA POSITIONS LOCATED AS
FOLLOWS FROM CENTER OF RUNWAY -- 2.8 NM NNW (5
EMPLACEMENTS OCCUPIED), 3.3 NM WSW (5 EMPLACEMENTS
OCCUPIED), 1.8 NM SW (4 EMPLACEMENTS OCCUPIED), AND
3.2 NM SSE (2 EMPLACEMENTS OCCUPIED).
AIRCRAFT -- 23 FAGOT/FRESCO AND ONE PROBABLE BEAST.
```

Extract of MCP report for GRC181 applicable to Saamcham AB describing its main features and the aircraft identified. (CIA)

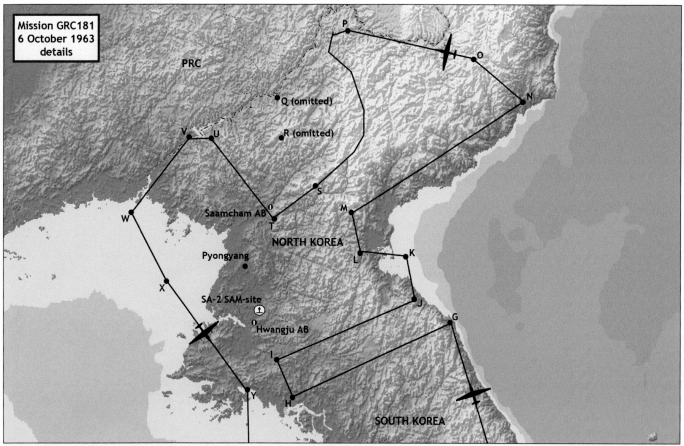

Wang's overflight route covered much of the DPRK but kept him clear of Pyongyang. (Map by Tom Cooper based on Data SIO, NOAA, USN, NGA, GEBCO and Landsat/Copernicus)

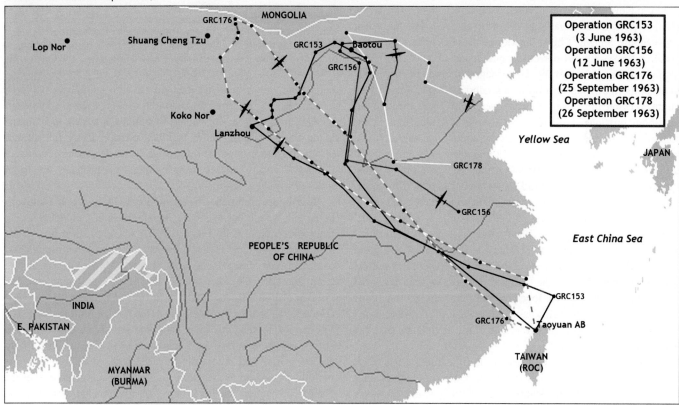

The intensity of the search across northern China looking for nuclear-related facilities saw four flights in June and September 1963 and included targets at Shuang Cheng Tzu, Koko Nor, Baotou and searching along the Yellow River. (Map by Tom Cooper based on Google Data SIO, NOAA, USN, NGA, GEBCO and Landsat/Copernicus)

Shuang Cheng Tzu, again from the north, then along the edge of Koko Nor, onto Lanzhou and Baotou also covering the industrial complexes around them. The post-mission report recorded only that minor changes had taken place at Shuang Cheng Tzu since the previous overflight, simply recording extensions to the railway network there.[34] What is not detailed is Mike Hua's recollection that near the target Wang's System XII illuminated several times. After he headed home continuous cloud cover prevented him from accurately ascertaining that he had passed out over the mainland coast until he was over the Pratas Islands, some 200 miles south-west of Taiwan after which he corrected course for Taoyuan arriving over an hour later than expected.[35]

Following several missions against the Shuang Cheng Tzu range area, the emphasis shifted towards the Lanzhou and Baotou enrichment plants. The former was Mike Hua's primary target for GRC153 on 3 June 1963. His route followed a clockwise loop to the north-east of Lanzhou as he followed the Yellow River's course for over 800nm, probably searching for additional nuclear processing locations that might have required large amounts of water to function. The final part of his route, before he headed for home, passed close to Baotou. Just nine days later, Mike Hua piloted GRC156 (12 June 1963) from Taoyuan. Flying to the far north, his main area of photographic interest was a roughly 140-mile west-east running strip, again following the Yellow River valley, from approximately where GRC153 had previously broken off following the river, close to Baotou.[36]

Attention returned to the missile range at Shuang Cheng Tzu five missions later with GRC176 on 25 September 1963. Pilot Nanping Lee took a direct route from Taoyuan, passed over Lanzhou, Koko Nor, Shuang Cheng Tzu, this time extending further north-west across its range area and then back towards Taiwan. This time Lee's imagery was assessed as 'excellent'. GRC178, flown by Changti 'Robin' Yeh, the following day, passed up through central China, again close to Baotou, before turning eastwards slightly north of the Yellow River and headed eastwards for roughly 200nm in a similar way to that of GRC153 back in June. He then turned southwards again as he approached the edge of Beijing and headed home.

On 1 November 1963, Changti 'Robin' Yeh flew Art 355 on Mission GRC184 and was shot down by an SA-2. His flight had revisited the Shuang Cheng Tzu range area. On the return leg, his aircraft's System XII detected a missile launch and gave him a high pitched audible warning. He managed to evade the first, only to have his right wing torn off by a second SA-2. He was only 40 minutes' flying time from Taiwan, over eight hours through his nine-hour mission. The detonation severely wounded him. Semi-conscious he baled out from the stricken aircraft. He only survived because Chinese doctors removed 53 major metal fragments, and many smaller pieces, from his lower body and gave him a blood transfusion. After a short period, he was removed to a PLA 'hostel' where he was kept in solitary confinement and interrogated over a prolonged period before being subjected to political 're-education'.

In summer 1965 'Cadre Zhao' (Robin Yeh's chief 'minder') accompanied by a soldier went from the Beijing PLA Air Force Hostel to the 'Military Museum of the Chinese People's Revolution'. Outside the building was the arranged debris from four destroyed U-2s. There they queued together with thousands of Chinese citizens for many hours to file past the wreckage, the crowd unaware that among them was a pilot from one of the 'spy planes' that had invaded Chinese airspace.[37]

Yeh was moved to live in a peasant farm commune where his highly educated status made him useful. Later his English skills opened an avenue to translation and teaching work. However, he remained a prisoner of the communists until 1982 when he was unexpectedly released, with colleague Major Chang and they crossed over the land border to Hong Kong.[38]

Following Yeh's loss, an immediate stand-down period saw the Taiwanese operated Det H U-2s finally fitted with some of the warning devices already installed in Agency aircraft elsewhere, including Birdwatcher. The US had been reluctant to supply this

Citizens queued for hours to view the wreckage of four shot down U-2s outside the Military Museum of the Chinese People's Revolution. Unknown to them on one such day U-2 pilot Robin Yeh, shot down on 1 November 1963, was queueing with them. (New China News Agency)

equipment, concerned that it might fall into communist Chinese hands. Missions restarted on 16 March 1964, but just six days later, on 22 March 1964, newly trained U-2 pilot Captain Thepei 'Sonny' Liang flew a coastal training/ELINT mission along the Taiwan Straits and disappeared. At some stage, he made a sharp manoeuvre in his U-2 and is believed to have broken up, probably due to an induced structural failure.

Overflights resumed in earnest from 26 June 1964 only to be subject to another loss on 7 July. Lieutenant Colonel Nanping Lee took off from Cubi Point as Mission C184C, part of a major combined operation.[39] Flying U-2G Art 362, he crossed the mainland coast between Hong Kong and Hainan. Meanwhile, departing from Taoyuan, Chenwen Wang left on his planned five-hour mission (C174C) to cover targets in Nanking, Wuhan, Hangshow (Hangzhou), Shangjao and Foochow (Fuzhou). A Taiwanese RF-101 Voodoo was tasked to fly a low-level coastal reconnaissance mission at the same time. A PRC SA-2 missile site had recently been set up at Changchow and reportedly tracked all three aircraft for short periods. At 1236 hours local time, the Taoyuan command post heard Nanping Lee report that his System XII activation light was flashing. Later it was discovered three missiles had been launched at him, at least one striking home. His aircraft came to earth seven miles west of the SA-2 site.[40] Lee's loss brought another halt to missions whilst new Taiwanese pilots were trained, extra aircraft procured and equipment fitted. Missions resumed on 31 October 1964.

Lanzhou

Although the Lanzhou site hosted a gaseous diffusion plant for enriching uranium, made obvious by the approximately 2,000ft long main plant building, it was also likely to be home for related activities. It became the centre of attention for combined space-based reconnaissance and U-2 missions. Mission C224C was a staged operation launched from Takhli at 0830 hours local on 31 October 1964 and flown by Liyi 'Jack' Chang, his first operational flight over the mainland. He used Art 352 and carried a B camera. Of his six hours 40 minutes airborne, he was in PRC airspace for five hours 20 minutes. Heavy cloud covered much of his route but fortunately broke over Lanzhou. There was no SAM activity identified but there was an attempted intercept by a MiG-19 'Farmer' aircraft approximately 95nm south-east of Sian (Xi'an, Xianyang airfield), which was even captured on his U-2's imagery.[41]

Whilst the B camera imagery was valuable, more sought after was intelligence that could reveal what was going on within the walls of the Lanzhou plant. Uranium processing operations generated considerable heat. It was decided to fly a series of night missions using an infrared camera. Referred to as the FD4 IR Scanner it had

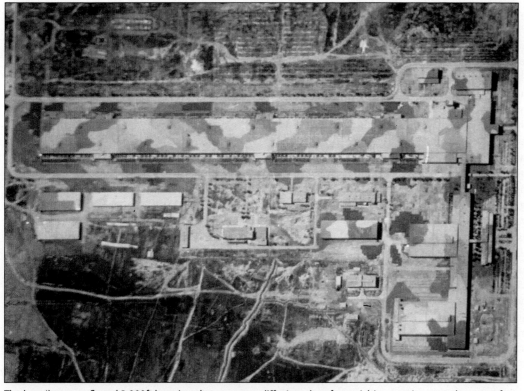

The heavily camouflaged 2,000ft long Lanzhou gaseous diffusion plant for enriching uranium was the target for many U-2 missions, with this image from a May 1966 KH-7 Gambit satellite pass. (CIA)

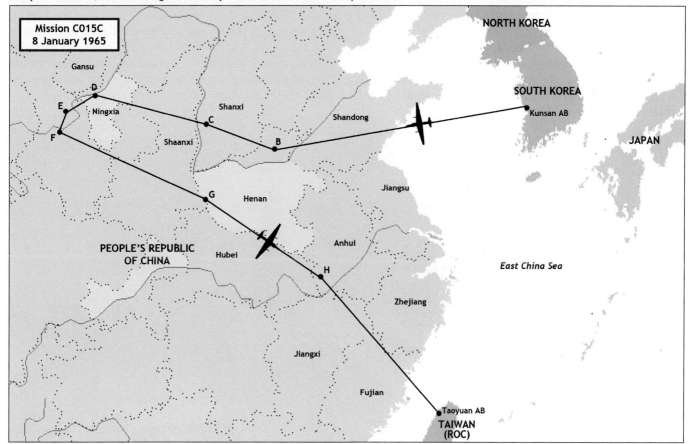

C015C on 8 January 1965 was a successful mission, after three earlier aborts, over the Lanzhou gaseous diffusion plant and used a Texas Instruments FD4IR infrared scanner to detect heat sources within it. (Map by Tom Cooper based on Google Data SIO, NOAA, USN, NGA, GEBCO and Landsat/Copernicus)

been developed by Texas Instruments, to image targets producing high 'thermal energy' signatures such as nuclear reactors. Two were purchased for U-2 use. They weighed 120lb, had a 100-degree field of view and produced a 28-mile-wide band of imagery at 70,000ft. Ultimately, the system was not particularly successful, with a 35ft space between objects necessary to achieve adequate resolution. The first mission carrying the FD4 IR took off on 22 November 1964 (Mission C284C), approximately 30 minutes after midnight from Kunsan AB in South Korea, flown by Liyi Chang. It made PRC landfall west of the Korean base and headed towards Lanzhou scheduled to recover to Taoyuan. But less than six hours later it had landed after experiencing problems with autopilot induced oscillations and more importantly an illuminated 'fail light' for the FD4. Mission C304C was launched three days later on 25 November 1964, flown by Pete Wang, probably from Kunsan again. His flight went smoothly until he was within about 30 miles of the Lanzhou plant when his System XII warning device indicated a missile launch and System XIII began jamming the SA-2. The brilliant flashes of light behind him indicated three missiles had exploded which temporarily ruined his night vision. He set course for home. A further mission (C344C) on 19 December 1964 aborted following the failure of its System XIII (a mandatory abort condition). Finally, Mission C015C on 8 January 1965 was successfully flown by Johnny Wang from Kunsan again. He headed directly to Lanzhou, flying over the plant from the north before setting course for the return to Taoyuan. In addition to his infrared scanner, he carried Systems VI, IXA, XII and XIII.[42]

Baotou Mission C025C

Having successfully used its infrared camera on Lanzhou attention turned again to Baotou with Mission C025C targeted at the uranium enrichment plant there on 10 January 1965, again using Art 358 with the FD4 infrared device. Pilot, Major Liyi 'Jack' Chang had flown one of the abortive attempts on Lanzhou the previous November. He departed Taoyuan at 1830 hours. The deeper he flew over the mainland the weaker his telemetry transmissions got. Finally, around 2120 hours, the Taiwanese ground stations lost contact altogether. As he later recounted, suddenly, without warning, his aircraft was struck by an SA-2:

When I had almost reached the target, a missile suddenly exploded nearby, with a blinding flash, breaking up the airplane. Neither System XII nor System XIII had shown me any sign of warning in advance. I was thrown out of the cockpit and lost consciousness. I did not know how long I had been falling through the sky. The jerk of the parachute automatically opening at about 14,000 feet above the ground woke me up, I felt excruciating pain in my right shoulder. The missile fragments must have pierced my flesh. My eyes were bloated as if almost falling out of their sockets. The missile fragments must have also damaged the capstans or oxygen hose of my pressure suit, which caused the suit to momentarily fail to protect me from the thin air of high altitude.

Major Chang's troubles were not over. He injured his ankles as he hit the frozen ground on landing. Having only his thin, close-fitting pressure suit, he was forced to wait out the night, with his parachute wrapped around him. A small search party with torches even passed close to him. After dawn, he saw nearby yurts to which he made his way. A woman there gave him some food and warmed him up, but as the wife of a local communist party official she sent for the militia while he slept. It took him three months to recover from his wounds. After interrogation and a lengthy period of solitary, he was briefly allowed to visit his mother and brothers in Nanjing in 1969. He had not seen them since he had left for Taiwan in 1947. He was later released to labour as a farm worker at a commune on condition he did not reveal he had been a U-2 pilot. He too was held in the PRC until 1982 when he was released with Robin Yeh.[43]

Chang's System XIII had failed to detect the missile, probably because the PRC technicians had adjusted the pulse repetition frequency of their SA-2's tracking radar, to defeat the U-2's defensive systems. That shortcoming was solved in the later modified System XIIIA which extended its frequency coverage. The loss caused recriminations within the Agency. Enquiries initially focussed on blaming NPIC for failing to detect and report the presence of new active SA-2 sites. NPIC was usually requested just before a mission to check within 50 miles of main targets and along the entry and exit routes for the presence of missile emplacements. They used a combination of previous U-2 and Corona satellite imagery. However, the quality of the satellite imagery was not always adequate to detect the sites. Even if detected, it was difficult or impossible to tell if SA-2s were really present and operational. The eventual findings led to the conclusion that it was one of two previously identified sites, one of which had fired on the Lanzhou mission, that brought Chang down, rather than a failure at NPIC.[44] In the wreckage of his aircraft, the Chinese found an intact 'black box' from the mounting

The wreckage of Major Liyi 'Jack' Chang's U-2C shot down on 10 January 1965. Seriously injured, he remained in the PRC until released in 1982. (Via Tom Cooper)

on the U-2's right wing slipper tank. The missile, or crash, had probably prevented the self-destruct mechanism activating. Established to be part of the U-2's self-defence system, from the box PRC technologists developed a counter-counter-measure system. They later claimed this was used to bring down Lungpei 'Tom' Hwang in September 1967.[45]

Taiwanese Takhli Missions
Using Takhli AB in Thailand offered opportunities to fly routes over southern China, entering PRC airspace from different directions to those possible from Taoyuan. This was done on several occasions by the Det H Taiwanese pilots. Still regarded as a sensitive issue, in most of the released CIA documentation to date they are often described as being flown from Taoyuan, or any mention of Takhli has simply been omitted.

In July 1961 the US 5412 Committee had insisted that missions over Vietnam be flown only by US pilots. However, by 1964, the position was slowly shifting. First, U-2 missions over Vietnam were becoming more 'tactical' in nature and most became a SAC responsibility. Second, the Taiwanese pilots had been on stand-down since their loss on 10 January 1965. Meanwhile, the list of priority targets requiring re-coverage was growing rapidly. In February 1965 the 5412 Committee approved the resumption of overflights and allowed TACKLE pilots more autonomy in the use of their System XIII jammer. An exchange of aircraft enabled three of the best-equipped airframes to be moved to Taoyuan. Det H was strengthened with extra personnel from Edwards AFB to enable simultaneous operations from both Taoyuan and Takhli. Agency staff commitments were changing too: just 130 were now fully committed to worldwide U-2 operations, 21 of them in Taiwan. The number dwindled as CIA involvement with the A-12 and National Reconnaissance Office (NRO) satellite programmes increased. An increased use of the Taiwanese pilots made practical sense. The Americans quietly relaxed their previous restriction on using non-US pilots to fly missions other than those launched and recovered from Taiwan.[46] However, Agency pilots continued to fly some operational missions against Cambodia, Laos and Vietnam up to 1974.

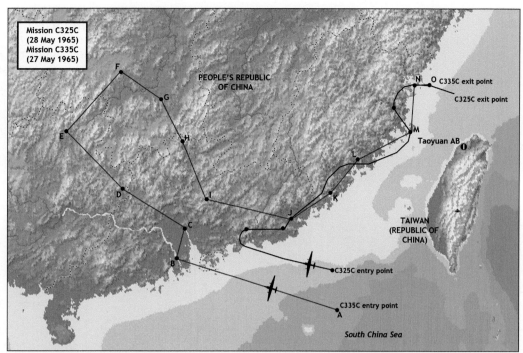

By 1965 overflight missions were planned in groups of three. C325C was largely a coastal overflight but C335C went some 300nm inland. (Map by Tom Cooper based on Data SIO, NOAA, USN, NGA, GEBCO and Landsat/Copernicus)

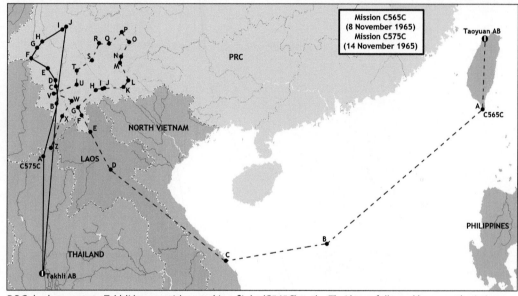

ROC deployments to Takhli began with a working flight (C565C) to the Thai base, followed by several missions before returning home. C575C aborted its mission over western PRC after its all-important 'Birdwatcher' system failed. (Map by Tom Cooper based on Google Data SIO, NOAA, USN, NGA, GEBCO and Landsat/Copernicus)

PRC Overflight Planning: 1965
Following the loss on 10 January 1965, Chinese mainland overflights resumed again on 19 February. For May 1965 another series of PRC overflights was planned. As was often now the habit, missions were planned in groups of three, expecting only two to take place. This was the case for Missions C315C, C325C and C335C. C315C and C325C were scheduled for 19 May 1965, with only one expected to fly, dependent on which had the best forecast weather. C315C was particularly ambitious, expected to fly over 300 miles inland from the PRC coastline. Penetration was to be near Macao and expected to remain in PRC airspace for over two hours. It was halted at the last moment. C325C was a less ambitious overflight from Shantou to Fu Chou (Fuzhou), largely adjacent to Taiwan, expected to be over PRC territory for just over one hour.

ANATOMY OF A NORTH KOREAN OVERFLIGHT

Planning individual overflights was an intricate process, with a large number of steps and lots of coordination. Whilst those procedures evolved the major elements were pretty constant from 1956. Outlining that process gives an insight into some of its complexity.

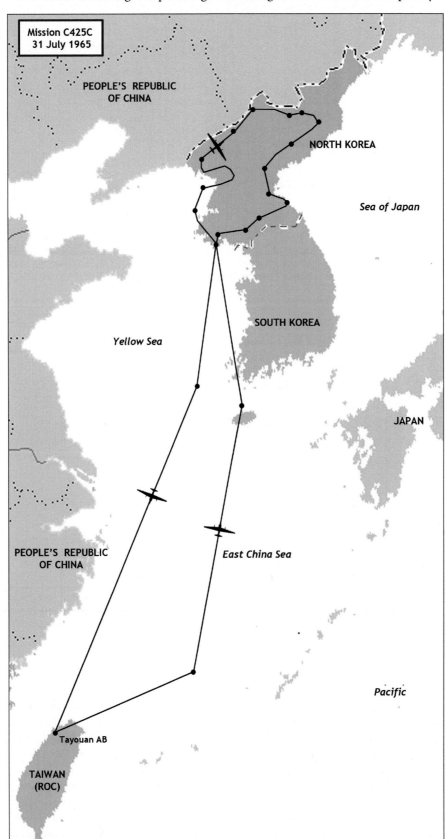

Mission C425C over North Korea was the first known to have imaged the Yŏngbyŏn nuclear reactor. (Maps by Tom Cooper based on Data SIO, NOAA, USN, NGA, GEBCO and Landsat/Copernicus)

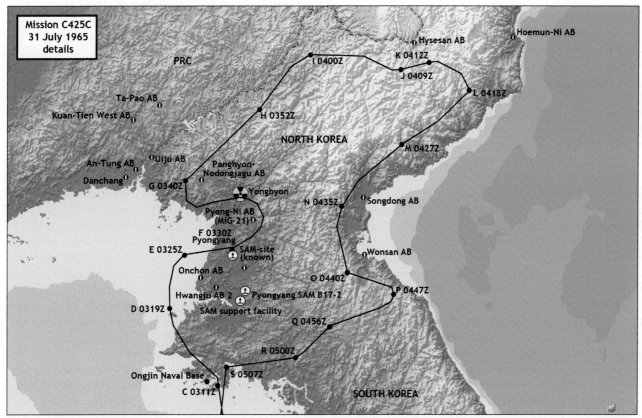

Close up of Mission C425C's route over North Korea. Its inland track into the North West of the DPRK allowed the Y4ngby4n nuclear facility to be imaged for the first time. (Maps by Tom Cooper based on Data SIO, NOAA, USN, NGA, GEBCO and Landsat/Copernicus)

The DPRK was not the highest priority target for US U-2 flights. They were irregular, often flown by Det H's Taiwanese pilots, such as: GRC128 (5 December 1962), C244C (7 November 1964) and C425C (31 July 1965). It is useful to explore this latter mission in detail, as it is a simpler one to explain. Nevertheless, it touches on all the major planning elements and contains a couple of twists.

Overflights of North Korea were intended to update the existing intelligence picture by discovering new targets of interest and charting any changes at previously identified sites. For C425C the target priority list was established by COMOR in February 1965, approved by the US Intelligence Board on 3 March 1965 and passed to the '303 Committee'. It was not unusual for the 303 Committee to be presented with several slightly different routes for their approval in case one or more were rejected. This gave the detachment alternative routes to suit different weather conditions. The Committee's approval might specify that, perhaps, only two flights were to be flown in a proposed three or four mission series, because their routes overlapped significantly. Approval of C425C was for the July programme. To permit sufficient time for the necessary coordination work, it often meant that specific dates might be agreed two to three months in advance. Alternatively, the approval might just specify the month in which they should be flown. The most detailed information for the mission implementation was closely held within the CIA's Office of Special Activities.

Mission dates had to avoid conflict with important presidential, or high-level political visits to the region, to avoid embarrassment if something went wrong. This could involve coordination with allies through military liaison arrangements, or friendly embassies, to secure mission overflight agreement.

A route was calculated by the mission planners. Those for the DPRK were relatively straightforward. It was essentially a self-contained area, geographically compact and relatively small. By 1965 most of its military bases and activities were already well known. Either they were periodically observed by satellite or by listening in on communications from specialised intelligence-gathering ships (like the ill-fated USS *Pueblo*); or by other collection flights and ground stations. The DPRK's domestic infrastructure was relatively simple, with few large cities, simple communication links, some heavy industry and agriculture across the country's difficult terrain.

The route calculated covered the highest priority targets, using as efficient and low-risk a route as possible. SA-2s were the major threats to the U-2, so their positions had to be identified and any changes to them regularly recorded.

To achieve high-quality imagery, targets were best photographed while the U-2 was flying straight and level. Images taken as the aircraft was turning risked looking 'smeared' and out of sharp focus. This meant turn points had to be carefully worked out. The U-2's arrival time over the highest priority targets was normally calculated to achieve the best photographic sun angles. This avoided images being seriously under or overexposed, with the sun at the most advantageous angle if possible.

Former USAF U-2 pilot Lieutenant Colonel Rick Bishop described the detailed mission planning process from the early 1980s. Although by that time the U-2Rs were carrying an inertial navigation system, the planning process was little changed from CIA days. He explained that 'Staff-Navigators were high ranking (Lt Col and Majors) when I entered the programme, some with CIA U-2 mission planning experience…It was a one-on-one

Continued on page 26

Continued from page 25

affair with the navigator and pilot. The navigator would draw up the navigation charts and fill in a 'Green Card' covering the coordinates of each Destination and Turn Point along the route.'[47]

Advanced notification to the detachments had to be sufficient to make the required preparations. A formal alert would be notified by cable via the HBJAYWALK system not less than 24 hours before the actual mission. 'This information includes take-off time, the general area of operation, equipment desired and special instructions as appropriate.' In practice, alerts were often passed several days in advance. 'Negative alerts' were also passed to detachments when an imminent mission launch was put on hold for any reason – mostly weather-related. The alerts were normally based on forecasts of clear weather over the target areas. They were generally prepared by a special security-cleared cell of the USAF Air Weather Service at Offutt AFB. Those forecasts were based on weather observations from thousands of points across the world, including Soviet sources, intercepted as they were transmitted across the USSR.

Take-off, transit and penetration times had to be coordinated with any SAR support involved, local radar suppression arranged, if required, and flights coordinated with other collection efforts such as RC-135s, specialist C-130s and ground stations if they were involved. The Joint Reconnaissance Centre in the US was responsible for overall coordination. The selected photographic processing facility would also be notified and arrangements for the immediate collection and transport of the exposed film put in place for high priority missions. Final preparations ensured:

Authority to launch the mission is provided to the detachment not less than two hours prior to take-off. At this time the information is also passed to supporting agencies as well as higher echelons of the Agency. A final re-check is made in Headquarters to see that political approval is still not affected by late-breaking developments.[48]

Mission C425C

This was calculated as a 2,603nm flight, estimated to last six hours 44 minutes, including one hour 56 minutes over denied territory. Penetration altitude was to be 69,000ft with a maximum of 71,000ft achieved as the fuel burned off and a 150-gallon fuel reserve. The aircraft was fitted with a B camera, plus Systems III, VI, IXB, XIIB, XIIIA and the OS warning device. The mission vulnerability estimate covered two known SA-2 SAM sites, south of Pyongyang, which had to be avoided by a minimum of 25nm. North Korean Air Force MiG-15s and MiG-17s were not considered a threat, but 14 MiG-21s, split between Pukchang-Ni and Pyong-Ni, were regarded more seriously. The National Photographic Intelligence Centre, once told of the planned route, checked through recent imagery for the presence of any 'previously unreported SAM sites'.[49]

Mission C425C was flown by Det H pilot Jaichuang 'Terry' Liu on 31 July 1965. His mission over North Korea was probably regarded as a relatively low-risk route for this, his first operational mission after completing training at Edwards AFB. Having received his final briefing, had his flight suit fitted and pre-

Weather in the target area is again reviewed and if satisfactory, the detailed mission plan is provided to the operating detachment not later than twelve hours before take-off. Included in the plan are detailed requirements including penetration times, altitudes, headings, targets, and camera flight lines. Also included are emergency instructions, authorized emergency landing bases in order of priority and any special information regarding survival, cover and friendly forces that may be pertinent to the mission. Hostile air and radar order of battle, etc., are also provided at this time to prepare for the pilot briefing.

A Go-No-Go decision was based on a final review of target weather and the:

The Yŏngbyŏn area in North Korea is home to its first nuclear reactor. This image is from Corona satellite KH-4A Mission 1023 from 26 August 1965. (Center for Strategic and International Studies CSIS)

This is an image of the Yŏngbyŏn reactor from Corona KH-4B Mission 1109 (4 March 1970). Its two J3 panoramic cameras had a resolution of six feet, much closer to the U-2's B camera. The reactor buildings stand out and the whole area looks far more 'settled' with features easier to identify than the image from August 1965. (CAST)

important early actor in the DPRK's nuclear history. A brief NPIC notification, less than two months before C425C, indicated the recent identification of 'An installation which is probably a nuclear research centre reportedly being constructed in the area … the most prominent feature of the installations a tall building with low bays on two sides. The building is similar in appearance to certain research reactor buildings observed in the Soviet Union, especially the one at Salaspils [Latvia].' This appears to be the most credible reason for the significant inland 'loop' Liu's mission route took as it passed up the west coast of the Korean peninsula.[51] Contained in the post-mission report was a sighting of a MiG-21 at 46,300ft around the Wonsan area.

A modified Soviet design 4-megawatt 'IRT-2000' research reactor was constructed at Yŏngbyŏn, North Korea's first, from mid-1964. The Centre for Strategic and International Studies' 'Beyond Parallel' project, presented by Joseph

breathed oxygen he was helped to get relatively comfortable in the cockpit.

He successfully took off from Taoyuan on time, at 0030Z (0830 hours local). Several addresses would be notified of his departure and later recovery by message via HBJAYWALK. Liu was in the air for seven hours and encountered slightly worse weather than predicted, mostly broken cloud. From a brief post-flight report he covered 33 COMOR targets comprising: 13 airfields, nine military installations, three naval facilities, one BW/CW centre, three electronic targets and four 'complexes'.[50] His imagery also caught two separate MiG-21 interception attempts as they flew beneath him. Post-flight imagery processing was completed by the 67th RTS at Yakota for in-theatre requirements and, via Eastman Kodak, to NPIC back in Washington DC for the main imagery. Distribution of the Initial Photographic Interpretation Report to around 40 recipients, for DPRK missions, at the time was not unusual. The exploitation of ELINT recordings was done by the Sobe Joint SIGINT processing facility on Okinawa and the Pacific Command ELINT centre at Fuchu.

The Mission Coverage Plot (MCP) logs 134 identified locations over North Korea, ten of which were new. Only one location is redacted. This is the Yŏngbyŏn research centre, an

Bermudez, contains an excellent detailed history of Yŏngbyŏn's origins.[52] It includes some good general images of the site's evolution from 1962 onwards, attributed to several Corona KH-4/4A missions.[53]

Sometimes the practice of 'sanitisation' would be used to remove any labels or marks from some selected imagery that would have identified it as coming from a higher-security classification. The photographs could then be downgraded to 'Top Secret', non-codeword status. As a result, it could be used by military cartographers and for inclusion in relevant bomber target folders. That there are few other targets identified from the MCP in the area of this loop strengthens the assertion that Yŏngbyŏn was the main reason for its inclusion in the mission route. It certainly served as a key target for reconnaissance satellites from that time on. If it was Jaichuang 'Terry' Liu's overflight, KH-4A Mission 1022, of 20 July 1965, or some other source that drew the attention of the US intelligence community to Yŏngbyŏn is as yet unidentified. Liu was one of just a handful of nationalist pilots who completed his ten operational missions tour-of-duty over denied territory.

Continued on page 28

Continued from page 27

The Yŏngbyŏn research reactor was the same Soviet design as that built at Salaspils, near Riga in Latvia in 1961. (via Pyotr Prokofyev)

to meet a requirement to cover fifty per cent of the North Korean targets quarterly and essentially all of them semi-annually. We have never been able to meet this requirement with the reconnaissance assets employed … The Committee has on several occasions reaffirmed the need for coverage of North Korea by the TACKLE programme. Because of conflicting priority and operational considerations, the TACKLE programme had not been able to provide the required coverage. North Korea was covered last by a U-2 on 31 July 1965 … Coverage by KH-4 has been useful to identify SAM sites, ground force installations, new construction etc and can provide air ORBAT information. It does not have adequate resolution, however, to provide ground force ORBAT and related military information.

In September 1967 the Chairman of COMIREX explained some of the shortcomings experienced in trying to collect imagery of the DPRK:

The intelligence community maintains a list of targets in North Korea of current intelligence concern. At present there are fifty-nine priority targets on this list … we have been attempting

These shortfalls were used to push the case to the US Intelligence Board (USIB) for early CIA BLACK SHIELD A-12 mission coverage of North Korea.[54]

At the last moment, flying the same route as the previously abandoned C315C, Mission C335C was substituted for C325C and flown on 27 May. C325C was rescheduled for the following day. High priority for the flights were new SA-2 sites. MiGs from five different airfields were scrambled against the U-2, each usually holding two aircraft on strip alert. Most were MiG-19s but there were concerns that a few MiG-21s had been moved to airfields in the region and might be ready to intercept the intruders. However, the risk of interception was assessed as below 12 percent. PRC fighters were spotted but appeared to be circling beneath the U-2 rather than attempting zoom climbs. Meanwhile, the ROC Air Force maintained combat air patrols over the Taiwan Straits.[55] The film from the two missions was regarded as the highest priority and whisked by C-130A 55-0032 to Eastman Kodak in New York for processing and evaluation.

Another group of missions were flown in November 1965. Each carried the same payloads: B camera, SIGINT Systems III and VI plus defensive systems IXB, XIIB and XIIIA. C565C departed Taoyuan on 8 November and made landfall over Da Nang in South Vietnam and headed north over Laos to cover targets in western China before landing at Takhli. However, its photographic coverage was limited by an early failure of the B camera. The next flight, C575C on 14 November covered a wide range of targets in a large part of western China. Flying a clockwise course, it aborted its mission after just over an hour over Chinese territory when its Birdwatcher system failed, and so returned to Thailand. The final mission was flown on 23 November following a very similar route to that planned for the aborted one but in an anticlockwise direction. In the intervening period, the unit flew a photographic survey of Thailand for its government.

From just these groups of flights, it is possible to see how rarely individual missions were completed without some significant issues, often with the cameras and the defensive aids. This was another reason why it was often necessary to schedule missions in small groups, over several days, to enable equipment failures to be rectified and allow for adequate photographic weather.

During 1966 US and nationalist mission priorities were becoming increasingly divergent. Satellites now led the coverage of the PRC's nuclear programme in northern China. American priorities for U-2 missions ranked, with the most important being overflights of southern China (because of Vietnam), followed in descending order by Manchuria, the PRC's east coast and the DPRK. The nationalists were more interested in the PRC ports and coastal airfields opposite Taiwan. Their second priority was a band of airfields, slightly further inland but still within range of the coast.[56] For the joint programme to continue these differing priorities had to be carefully balanced.

Unfortunately, attrition continued. During 1966 ten successful overflights were marred by two fatal losses in training accidents.[57] The first of Major Tseshi Wu on 17 February 1966. The heavy losses were beginning to affect nationalist confidence in the programme. After the presentation of the accident report on the 21 June 1966 loss of Major Chingchang Yu in Art 384, during a training flight, the nationalist's recriminations surfaced over the quality of pilot training and aircraft maintenance.[58]

By 1966 losses and retirements meant there was a need for a significant number of new pilots to be trained on the U-2. In June 1966 Taiwanese U-2 pilot training was moved from Davis-Monthan AFB in Arizona to Edwards AFB alongside Detachment G and the British. As within the CIA, the Taiwanese pilot selection process was always a very secretive one. Only pilots with 'outstanding records' were to be selected and told only that they had been 'selected to be trained in high-performance aircraft in the US'. After selection, the training syllabus for Taiwanese U-2 pilots involved some 70 hours of ground school. That was preceded by some flight time in the T-33 with instructors to get them used to USAF/FAA and local procedures around Edwards AFB. Once ground school was completed lucky students would get a pair of flights in a two-seat U-2. Otherwise, it was a standard U-2. In both cases the training involved practice at low altitude turns, handling in the approach to stalling and five take-offs and landings. These were accompanied by a T-33 or U-3 chase plane. The main flight syllabus required a minimum of 55 flight hours spread across 15 sorties.[59]

In 1967 there were another 12 U-2 missions, mostly against southern China and the Taiwan Straits. An 8 September 1967 flight, Mission C297C (Art 373), resulted in another SA-2 loss, this time approximately 75 miles south-west of Shanghai with pilot Jungpei Hwang being killed. Soon after he crossed the mainland coast on his first operational mission, his OS system operated but even with evasive manoeuvring, his aircraft was fatally hit. Later the PRC claimed they had used an ECCM system to overcome the System XIIIA jammer he carried said to have been recovered from the wreckage of Liyi Chang's shootdown.[60]

Desert Drops

The nuclear testing grounds at Lop Nor in northern China were established in 1959. They covered nearly 40,000 square miles and were naturally of great intelligence interest. It became the target for two remarkable missions in 1967. Two CIA reports reveal their routes. Beyond the U-2's range from Taiwan, they were staged from Takhli. As they required a special mission fit the two modified aircraft were ferried from Edwards to Hawaii (by Squadron Leaders Martin Bee and Bazil Dodd), Guam and finally Takhli in April. Crossing the Pacific they were supported by a KC-135A that also provided en route SAR.[61] The deployment to Takhli was done in considerable secrecy to hide the extra activity as much as possible. Once on the ground in Thailand personnel were asked to ensure the presence of the two extra U-2s was as discreet as possible to avoid questions about why they were there. Even with this forward staging operation, it was still more than a 3,000-mile round trip. Operating close to the U-2's extreme range, they inevitably followed about 90 percent similar routes. Half the flight was inside PRC airspace.

The first (C167C) launched on 7 May 1967. Art 383 was flown by pilot 'Spike' Chuang. Its normal main camera was replaced with an extra fuel tank installed in the Q-bay. A T-35 tracker camera was fitted to record the actual flight route. His electronic suite consisted of Systems III, VI, IXB, XIIB, XIIIC, and 'Oscar Sierra'.

Mission departure time for C167C was important because it was calculated to ensure that when the U-2 dropped its pods the sun would be at a good angle to ensure that the tracker camera recorded the precise drop zone. Unfortunately, the tracker camera failed to work, part of the mechanism being frozen as it was not turned on until two hours into the flight. Alarmingly, Chuang experienced heavy contrailing for roughly 500nm as he approached the Himalayas lasting until he was clear of them. Accordingly, he made random minor course changes between Points B and D on the lookout for fighters. He pressed on, even though contrailing was a specified mission abort condition.

His payload was two underwing mounted remote sensors, developed by the Sandia Laboratories in conjunction with the CIA for the Lop Nor flight.[62] The pylons on which the sensors were to be fitted were those used when extra drop tanks were fitted – not

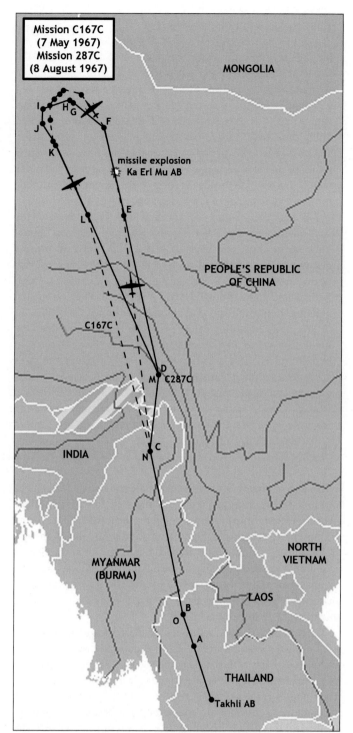

Missions C167C and C287C were very ambitious operations to drop remote monitoring equipment in the desert near the Lop Nor nuclear testing ground. (Map by Tom Cooper based on Data SIO, NOAA, USN, NGA, GEBCO and Landsat/Copernicus)

to be confused with the slipper tanks carried for most long-range missions. To safely accommodate the pylons the slipper tanks were removed. Although the fuel they could have carried was badly needed, there were worries that they would adversely affect the aircraft's performance. Precise navigation was aided by two specially installed Doppler navigation sets. The pods were dropped over the testing grounds between waypoints G and I. First the left wing pod, then the right 49 seconds later. The payload's nose was intended to pierce the desert surface and transmit unspecified data at regular intervals. Chuang reported not jettisoning the pylons themselves until he was 'well into a mountainous area'. He omitted waypoint D outbound and M on his return. This meant he briefly passed through

DEVELOPING THE 'POD'

During July 1966 Lockheed was contracted to undertake the research, development and test work for an airdropped remote sensor to be completed by 1 March 1967. Two aircraft were selected and modified for the task. Art 383 was to be the primary aircraft with Art 373 as a 'last resort' reserve. Modifications included fitting a fuel tank in the Q-bay replacing the main payload space. The pods were to be carried on external pylons fitted in the same positions on the U-2's wings as those used for carrying the rarely seen U-2 drop tanks. Inside the cockpit, electronics were installed to test the functioning of the payload once it was dropped.

No confirmed pictures or drawings have yet emerged of the payload dropped at Lop Nor. They have been described as 'spikes', 'rock radar' and 'pods' in some of the declassified documents discovered. The contracted work included constructing the real pods, plus dummies and eight pylons for their external carriage. Several test flights from Edwards AFB practised releasing the pods and testing the explosive bolts that jettisoned the pylons.

We get an indication of the pod's size from a cable detailing its dimensions to allow packaging crates for their shipment to be constructed. This describes the 'spikes' – probably the most accurate description – as weighing around 285lb, being 8.75in in diameter and approximately 120in long. The pylons and devices were also made 'sterile' which meant removing any identifying marks or labels that could have enabled their origin to be traced back to the US.

Agency documents indicate there was some uncertainty about whether the devices were to be powered by battery packs or solar 'petals'. The selection of the power supply made some difference to the aft design of the pods as they probably needed some fin arrangement to ensure they dropped vertically after release. The pods were to be ready by 1 March 1967 but it appears that the final selection of the solar-powered option was not made until 17 April.[63]

Mike Hua has described the objects as being 15ft long, which suggests the tail assembly was 5ft long. He has described that the nose of the device was to penetrate the desert surface when solar panel 'petals' would deploy to power the sensors and act as an antenna to transmit unspecified data to a receiving station in Taiwan at specific times.[64] What data the pods, described as 'transponders', transmitted remains unstated, but was most probably seismic data to detect an atomic weapon explosion. The PRC's first H-bomb exploded at Lop Nor on 17 June 1967.

After the failure to receive transmissions in July 1967 'pod unit #3' was to be 'imbedded' approximately six feet into the ground, near the end of a runway (probably Edwards AFB), clear of obstructions and placed under guard. Presumably, this was to try and see if it could be remotely activated. There is no report available on how this test progressed.

Indian airspace but this shortened the route and reduced total flight time to a still exhausting eight hours 45 minutes. This was important given the extreme mission distance and that he was 50 gallons below the fuel curve, attributed to higher winds and contrailing. Although the sensors were successfully dropped over Lop Nor and activated no response was detected. During the mission a C-130 was airborne, equipped as a recovery team should, perhaps, the now appropriately nicknamed 'Spike' Chuang have to divert with a fuel or other emergency to an undisclosed airfield.

The data from the pod received in Taiwan was unsatisfactory so a second flight was authorised. On 31 August 1967 Mission C287C was piloted by Hsieh 'Billy' Chang and used Art 383 again. This time his payload was a High-Frequency trailing-wire antenna to ascertain if the 'pods' were working. He remained in the Spike drop area for ten minutes to tune up the communication between the remote sensor and the station in Taiwan. He then resumed course.[65] The mission was a near disaster when he was targeted by an SA-2 system, set along the outward leg of his route. Chang reported brief activity on his XIIIC, XIIB and Oscar Sierra systems, during which he sighted two missile contrails. The 'pilot initiated evasive action and after approximately 20 to 30 seconds observed two explosions'. He expected to fly the route with entry at 60,000ft climbing to 67,000ft by the exit. An SA-2 exploded just 2,000 to 3,000ft below and off the left of his aircraft; another at a similar height and a few thousand feet behind the right side of his U-2. At the time he was close to Ka Erh Mu airfield, around 300 miles south-south-east of Lop Nor. Identifying the exact interception location was difficult because of an undercast and a problem with the tracker camera. Chang believed four missiles were launched at him.[66] His flight lasted nine hours six minutes and covered 3,295 miles. Unfortunately, his antenna detected no signals from the 'pods'. A later operation, using C-130s, eventually put different remote sensors in place.

Slowing Overflights

The original Project Razor agreement in 1961 had specified the responsibilities of the US and nationalist governments connected to U-2 operations from Taiwan. In March 1967 there was a revision to that agreement through which the Taiwanese sought to reduce the possibility of a sudden unilateral American withdrawal from U-2 operations.[67] Just a few months later in October 1967, the US decided to halt its CIA/Taiwanese P-2V mainland unconventional warfare operations, which considerably soured US–Taiwanese relations. That cooling was softened somewhat by a US promise to upgrade the U-2's defensive aids and the possible introduction of the new H camera, then under development, plus improved SIGINT equipment.

Another northern coastal mission was flown on 13 December 1967 (C297C). That was followed by another on 5 January 1968 (C018C) which paralleled the mainland coast to the north of Taiwan. Although technically an overflight (it infringed PRC coastal airspace) it was a test for what soon became a wholly peripheral reconnaissance programme.[68] Both were early H camera flights. Mission C058C on 16 March 1968 was the last U-2 overflight of China, mounted from Takhli, and covered part of south-west PRC, south of Kunming and border areas of Laos, Burma and North Vietnam. It brought back 5,970ft of exposed film, representing 3,980 frames having flown for 538 miles over the PRC of its 1,694-mile flight and covered a remarkable 40,888 square miles of its territory.[69]

By April 1968, the US was absorbed with the Vietnam war and actively trying to improve relations with the PRC. Faced with a growing shortage of U-2 airframes and increased availability of better-quality satellite imagery, the '303 Committee' decided to halt overflights of the PRC. The termination saw a switch to peripheral only missions, the first on 18 May 1968. These were mixed photographic and SIGINT flights using the one remaining

Mission C018C

This U-2R mision was technically an overflight of the Chinese mainland's coastal belt, adjacent to Taiwan on 5 January 1968.

It came after the halt to deep penetration missions following the shooting down of Capt Lungpei (Tom) Huang on 8 September 1967 by an SA-2. C018C was only the third operational use of the new H camera. The route was a form of test flight for the peripheral flight programme that began on 8 April 1969 which flew a minimum of 20 miles off the coast.

Art 383 took-off from Taoyuan at 2100Z flying north eastwards until reaching Hangzhou Bay, (just south of Shanghai). He then turned to fly back over the mainland coast. Along his route he imaged 33 COMIREX designated targets and a further 29 'bonus' ones. In doing so he covered 1341 miles landing back at Taoyuan 4hrs 10mins later. This flight took 4438 images.

This image is a composite of the maps used to show the Mission Coverage Plot for C018C.

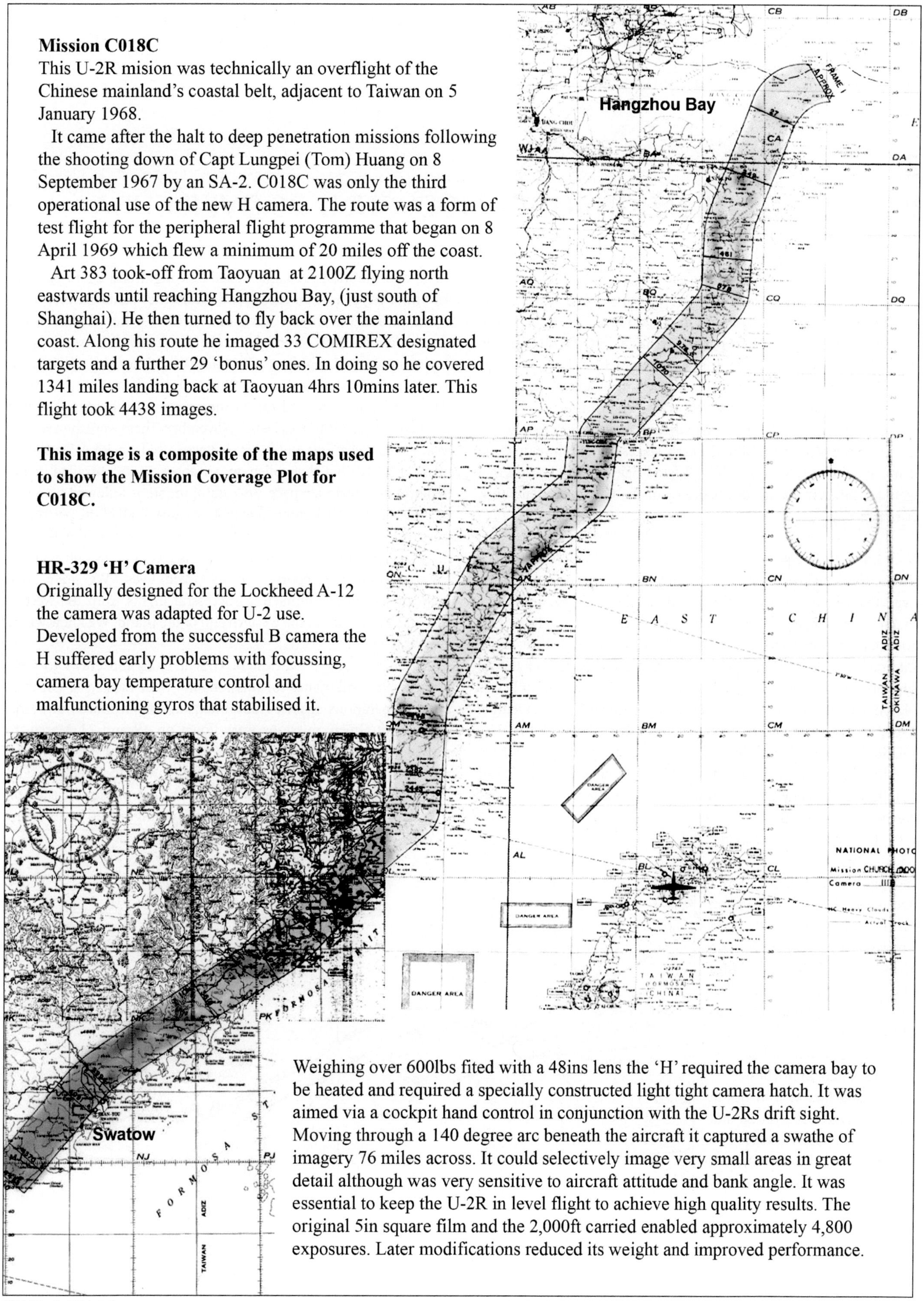

HR-329 'H' Camera

Originally designed for the Lockheed A-12 the camera was adapted for U-2 use. Developed from the successful B camera the H suffered early problems with focussing, camera bay temperature control and malfunctioning gyros that stabilised it.

Weighing over 600lbs fited with a 48ins lens the 'H' required the camera bay to be heated and required a specially constructed light tight camera hatch. It was aimed via a cockpit hand control in conjunction with the U-2Rs drift sight. Moving through a 140 degree arc beneath the aircraft it captured a swathe of imagery 76 miles across. It could selectively image very small areas in great detail although was very sensitive to aircraft attitude and bank angle. It was essential to keep the U-2R in level flight to achieve high quality results. The original 5in square film and the 2,000ft carried enabled approximately 4,800 exposures. Later modifications reduced its weight and improved performance.

(CIA/Kevin Wright)

U-2C. They were certainly more cautious missions, restricted to a 20-mile closest approach distance, later extended to 25 miles, from the coast.[70] Another loss occurred on 5 January 1969 during one such peripheral flight. The autopilot of Hsieh 'Billy' Chang's U-2G

(Art 385) failed in very turbulent conditions and caused him to bale out over the Pacific where immediate SAR operations failed to find him.[71]

3
WATCHING THE NEIGHBOURHOOD: CIA U-2S OVER CUBA

The loss of Gary Powers on May Day 1960 and U-2 flights over Cuba during the missile crisis in October 1962 are the two events that brought the most direct and international public attention to U-2 operations. The CIA in particular has a very dark history in its activities relating to Cuba. It has broken many careers, not least that of CIA Deputy Director for Plans, Richard Bissell. An extremely talented man, he was a key driving force behind getting the U-2 into service working with designer Kelly Johnson and others like Edwin Land. He was also involved in the early stages of A-12 development. It was his major role in the 1961 ill-fated Bay of Pigs invasion that would ultimately see his departure from the CIA and later public criticism.

Kick Off and Green Eyes

Before the Cuban missile crisis, CIA U-2s had been in operation over the island for some time. Colonel Stan Beerli, himself a major character in U-2 operations and previously Detachment B's commander, was well versed in planning missions with a major international dimension. He later headed a major part of the air support element for the Bay of Pigs operation and was naturally well placed to take advantage of the Agency's U-2 capabilities. In October 1960, Det G commenced Operation 'Kick Off', the CIA's first U-2 missions against Cuba. They were staged through Laughlin AFB, Del Rio, Texas home of the USAF's U-2A equipped 4080th Wing. It followed the now-familiar 'quick move' model with a U-2 and Agency C-54 as support. Their cover was as an operational readiness test for staging operations. Kick Off was carried out independently of all the USAF's specialist U-2 facilities sitting on the same airfield. The team involved just 15 people, two U-2s with civilian markings and the 'Go Kit' in a C-54. The mission photographic take was to be flown back to Edwards in the U-2, removed and sent by C-54 to Kodak in Rochester.

Al Rand flew two sorties in Art 353 over Cuba on 26 and 27 October 1960 (3001 and 3002) to try and collect ORBAT intelligence and identify potential landing zones for assault and airdropped forces. These long-range flights, of around 3,500nm took over nine hours. Even with slipper tanks, they were at close to maximum

range and duration.[1] A fault on the first flight and cloud cover of the entire target area for the second meant they achieved very little.

As invasion planning advanced, three further flights, code-named 'Green Eyes', were far more productive. These involved deployments to Laughlin AFB again, this time with 'drivers' Al Jones, Jim Cherbonneaux and Buster Edens. Art 342, a 'Hibal' (U-2C version) was used for all the successful missions. The first successful flight (3003) was on 27 November. There were then several weather cancellations until Art 343 was used on its 4 December mission (3010) but that called an 'air abort' as it contrailed before penetrating Cuban airspace. Successful missions followed on 5 and 13 December 1960. Equipped with its B camera, all of the peripheral missions were able to produce interpretable imagery of the island in the absence of obscuring cloud cover. As Det G's new commander, Colonel William Gregory, said of Green Eyes: 'We pretty well mapped the place, completing successful flights from the west to east and back again to the western end of the island. We knew where everything was.'[2]

In January 1961 Detachment G sent U-2s and crews to Cubi Point in the Philippines for missions in South East Asia. On their return, operations against Cuba intensified from March onwards. Two 'Long Green' missions were flown on 19 and 21 March, to provide the latest ORBAT update on Cuba. From 6 to 29 April missions accelerated sharply over the island, with 15 Operation 'Flip Top' flights, flown daily from just before the Bay of Pigs invasion on 7 April to the abandonment of the failed landings on 20 April. Using

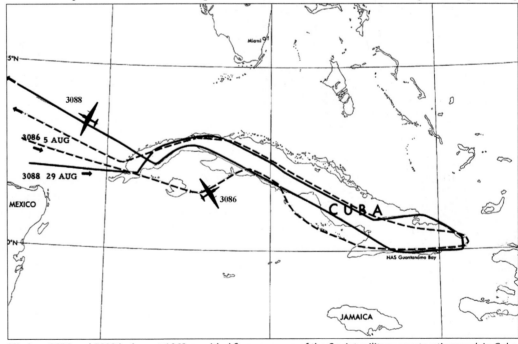

Missions 3086 and 3088 in August 1962 provided firm coverage of the Soviet military construction work in Cuba. The missions were 24 days apart because of continual bad weather. (Based on CIA map)

just two aircraft for these missions, Art 344 and 378, they fulfilled a more tactical than strategic role.[3]

Nimbus and the Cuban Crisis

In May 1961 the emphasis on Cuba shifted back to more strategic missions grouped under the project name 'Nimbus', and another seven, flown by Detachment G over the island up to the end of 1961. Cherbonneaux's Mission 3048 flown on 23 May 1961, took off from Edwards, overflew Naval Air Station (NAS) Corpus Christi, where it was refuelled by a KC-135A, on to Cuba and returned to Laughlin.[4] In total, Det G flew 24 missions over Cuba in 1961 and another 21 the following year.

Through early 1962 Cuban missions continued on a two flights per month basis. On at least two occasions, precautionary diversion landings were made on the return leg from Cuba. On 19 January 1962 Art 344 diverted to NAS Key West, following a DC generator failure. Mission 3079 went to England AFB, LA on 22 May 1962, with a low fuel warning. Det G's resources were becoming heavily stretched with continuing commitments over Cuba and a further series of flights in South East Asia. Splitting men and machines between two very distant locations, nearly 10,000 miles apart, made operations even more complicated.

The continuing regular U-2 surveillance of Cuba provided ORBAT updates of the island. During 1962 NPIC photographic interpreters began to see visible physical changes to Cuban military equipment and infrastructure. As the year wore on the scale of new construction became more obvious. U-2 overflights continued providing strategic intelligence of developments in conjunction with other covert and overt intelligence sources. Photographic interpreters and analysts had already compiled a comprehensive 'library' of eastern bloc military infrastructure from U-2 overflights in Europe. Using direct comparison, they were well equipped to identify most of what was being constructed by Soviet engineers in Cuba, from its very early stages, before it was even completed.

The turning point was the identification of possible SA-2's SAMs in Cuba, during Ericson's Mission 3088 on 29 August 1962. That was of immediate importance because of the proven threat they posed to the U-2. Overnight, it removed their invulnerability to existing Cuban air defences. More importantly, it raised the question of why deploy them? New SA-2 sites were likely an early indicator of other impending developments. SA-2s were frequently used to protect areas housing high-value assets, including nuclear-related facilities. Indeed, that was the view taken by the now DCI John McCone. The search was on for what the SA-2s would protect.

Agency U-2 missions remained relatively cautious peripheral flights, because of fears about adverse public attention if an incident took place. A very different attitude soon took over. When Mission 3088 confirmed SAM site construction on 29 August 1962 coverage was quickly stepped up, at the request of COMOR. The first took place on 5 September when Mission 3089, flown by Buster Edens found three more SAM sites, and a MiG-21 at Santa Clara AB, with more waiting to be un-crated. The weather during much of September was generally very poor; however, the CIA successfully mounted three more flights, in another forward based operation from Laughlin AFB. These flights: 3091, 3093 and 3095 all produced total coverage on 17, 26 and 29 September respectively, which revealed growing numbers of SA-2 sites. These long-range missions from Laughlin were mainly flown by U-2F Art 343 backed by Art 342. They were air refuelled by KC-135A with mission times lasting around seven hours. Up to three tankers were stationed at McCoy AFB in Florida to support the U-2F flights, part of a larger tanker presence at McDill AFB.[5] The pressure continued on the CIA to mount more peripheral missions. However, persistent bad weather put a hold on more flights: between 5 and 26 September, only one mission was able to be flown.[6]

As the crisis over Cuba deepened, the Joint Chiefs of Staff increased pressure on Defence Secretary Robert McNamara to start overflight missions and transfer responsibility for U-2 operations to SAC, which he did. The last two Agency missions were again

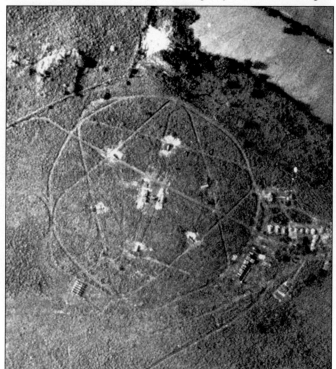

Bob Ericson's Mission 3088 on 29 August 1962 detected the construction of SA-2 sites at several locations including one near Havana and another near La Coloma. Their distinctive 'Star of David' layout had already become familiar to photographic interpreters since first seen close to the Berlin Corridors in East Germany some years before. (CIA)

peripheral flights. On 5 October, Jim Barnes flew a nine-hour mission (3098) along Cuba's southern coast in Art 343. The flight was to be supported by two USAF Air Rescue Service Grumman SA-16 Albatrosses. They flew roughly parallel to the southernmost part of the U-2's route, along the Cuban coast but around 20nm offshore. They kept a listening watch on the UHF distress frequency in case the U-2 got into trouble. There were two designated refuelling brackets, one over Key West and the other slightly further north over the Everglades where the mission could be met by a KC-135A flying at 35,000ft. NAS Key West was also to provide unspecified fighter support within its range.[7] The following day Jim Baker abandoned a similar north coast peripheral mission, 3099, when the slipper tanks failed to feed fuel properly

Continuing the pattern, the CIA's last two flights were again peripheral missions. Mission 3101 was SAC's first overflight and reflected the change to using military pilots in a more overtly assertive overflight mode. (Based on CIA map)

on Art 342. Marty Knutson flew the final Agency mission, 3100 (Art 343) on 7 October, a redo of the previous day's planned flight.

The transfer of responsibility was approved by President Kennedy on 12 October 1962 as pressure on the Cubans became more overt and overflights rapidly increased: six flights alone on 17 October, a total of 17 in their first week of operations.[8] By most measures, the transfer made sense to reflect the more intensive, closer to the tactical role now required. From another perspective, it disrupted existing planning, command and control arrangements. Certainly, the transfer to SAC operations was rushed.

As tensions rapidly escalated, nearly sparking a nuclear war, SAC U-2 overflights became a vital part of US management of the crisis. An immediate problem arose with the fact that USAF aircraft were U-2As and not the more modern and higher-flying U-2C/Fs, with their better J-75 engines. Two Air Force pilots Steve Heyser and Rudolph Anderson were quickly updated on the new variant and qualified on the U-2C by Agency pilots back at Edwards AFB.

Arrangements were made for SAC to use McCoy AFB in Florida as a much closer staging base, supported by some Det G personnel.[9] This greatly shortened the missions, with the first SAC flight on 14 October, originally planned as Det G Mission 3101. They continued to use the same Agency U-2Fs, Art's 342 and 343 now loaned to the USAF.[10] On 14 October, Steve Heyser's flight discovered the installation of Soviet nuclear Medium Range Ballistic Missiles (MRBMs) at St Cristobal, where 3088 had first imaged the SAMs on 29 August. Once that discovery was made it became a full-grown crisis and SAC was authorised to launch as many U-2 missions as were required. These were supplemented by low-level USAF RF-101C and USN RF-8A Crusader photographic reconnaissance missions. Less than 14 days later on 27 October 1963, Major Rudolph Anderson was flying Art 343 over Cuba when he was shot down and killed. Whilst elements of the missile crisis played out

very publicly, Detachment G's involvement in the early stages of the aerial reconnaissance remained in the shadows for some time.

U-2 v Corona over Cuba

One of the acid tests of photographic reconnaissance is, does it tell you what you need to know? During the Cuban missile crisis, a KH-4 Corona satellite was tasked to generate imagery of Cuba and serves as a useful qualitative comparison point between U-2 and satellite imagery of the day.

The decision was taken by COMOR to use a Corona satellite, to image the western part of Cuba, already identified from the previous Agency U-2 missions, as the most developed part of the island and home to the majority of its military infrastructure. COMOR was well aware of the limitations of Corona imagery compared to the U-2, but its invulnerability was a decisive factor.

Corona Mission 9045 lifted off from Vandenberg AFB on 29 September 1962. On its thirtieth orbit of the earth, it passed over western Cuba. Having looked over the imagery, academic Joseph Caddell has described that just frames 11 to 22 covered the western end of Cuba, which was partially obscured by cloud. This imagery was described in a later PFIAB chronology of the crisis: 'the resulting photography was good by Corona standards, but not of sufficient quality to reflect significant photographic intelligence on MRBM or IRBM developments on the island'.[11] It was not just that the KH-4's camera resolution was insufficient to see the missiles themselves, it was not detailed enough to identify the host of vital support vehicles and other equipment required by the SS-4 and SS-5 missile systems in the field.

Mission 9045 was in space for less than 72 hours before the film capsule was jettisoned as it passed close to Kodiak, Alaska and snatched out of the air near Hawaii by a modified C-119 from the 6953rd Test Squadron on 2 October 1962. Returned to Hickam AFB, the film capsule was immediately flown to the US, processed

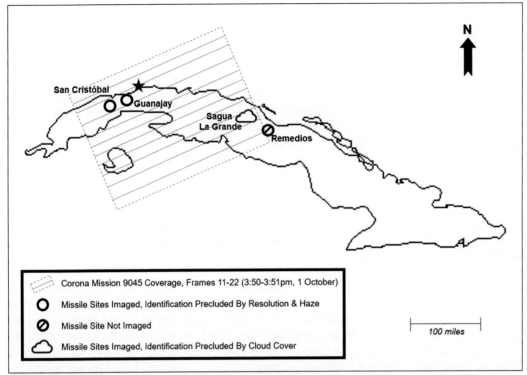

N

Corona Mission 9045 Coverage, Frames 11-22 (3:50-3:51pm, 1 October)

○ Missile Sites Imaged, Identification Precluded By Resolution & Haze

⊘ Missile Site Not Imaged

☁ Missile Sites Imaged, Identification Precluded By Cloud Cover

100 miles

The extent of key target coverage over Cuba by Corona Mission 9045, with most obscured by cloud. This was the only satellite coverage of the crisis. (Joseph Caddell, 'Corona over Cuba')

was not possible to cover all of Cuba in a single mission. It was a pre-programmed system over which no control could be exercised once launched. The U-2 had much greater flexibility in target selection and timing. Whilst re-planning U-2 operations was an expensive process, rearranging a Corona launch was many times more complex and took much longer to do. Neither could Corona photographic material be recovered, processed and assessed in the same timescale as U-2 imagery. Time-critical intelligence was much more likely to remain useful if it was collected by the U-2. However, the considerable advantages of U-2 imagery had to be balanced against the risk to its pilots once SA-2 sites became operational.

After the crisis had ended, SAC photographic interpreters later re-examined the Corona Mission 9045 imagery and determined that it was not possible to identify the SA-2s and other key sites from the space-based imagery.[13] This was a clear limitation on the value of Corona photography until its quality significantly improved. Over the next few years, the CIA and NPIC used Corona's wide-area coverage, particularly of the PRC, as an aid to identify locations for further U-2 missions. As the Corona coverage improved it enabled NPIC interpreters to more accurately identify possible SA-2 sites along the routes of planned U-2 missions.

and the finished images despatched from there. Cuba was not the main objective of Mission 9045 – gathering imagery of Sary Shagan and Kamchatka peninsula was. The satellite was programmed to pass over those targets when the sun was in an optimal position for image collection. The pass over Cuba just had to fall in with the planning for the primary targets. The PIs that would have poured over the photography, believed to be from the 544th RTG at SAC HQ, would have concentrated on the Soviet imagery first before looking at the Cuba coverage. The NPIC report for Mission 9045 appears not to have been prepared until 7 October 1962 and so the data was likely already a minimum of seven days old when they examined it. Hardly current by that stage.[12]

Although Corona images produced wide-area coverage, there was no flexibility in what they covered. Its orbit pattern meant it

Operations targeting Cuba put considerable pressure on the aircraft, pilots and members of Detachment G for two years from October 1960 to 1962. However, this was just part of their worldwide deployment commitment, to which were added training and test responsibilities.

4
DET G: WANDERING THE WORLD

Edwards AFB was an important location for CIA U-2 activities. Among the vast amount of open and classified research and test work undertaken there during the 1950s to 1970s, CIA and Air Force U-2 operational and training activities were largely hidden in plain sight. Forced out of Watertown, when the Atomic Energy Commission wanted to renew nuclear testing in Nevada, the CIA and USAF evacuated the remote desert site by 21 June 1957. The massive facility that is Edwards AFB, was the USAF's main test and research field, and HQ of Air Research and Development Command. New construction work soon created a secure area, renovated hangar and support facilities for the U-2. Initially, it was used for testing equipment, plus the development and installation of special equipment fits, working with Lockheed's Palmdale plant.

Major early programmes included testing the Project Rainbow modifications, to make the U-2 more 'stealthy' and development of the C camera, until it too was abandoned. Another was trialling airframe modifications and testing the J-75 engine to replace the original J-57s that increased the U-2's operating ceiling and payload performance. One-off equipment fits, such as System VII to Art 344, which enabled tracking of Soviet ICBM launches, were installed and tested between Lockheed and Edwards before it was deployed operationally.

Less obvious work included the reduction of electronic noise to improve the performance of SIGINT equipment, developing an improved pilot oxygen system, a leaflet drop device, dropping simulated photo-satellite payloads for airborne recovery tests and much more. There were special modifications that took the U-2 to sea, operating from US Navy aircraft carriers. Another enabled a few U-2s to aerial refuel, considerably extending their operational range.

Edwards was also the training location for Taiwanese and British U-2 pilots.

Edwards' operational role was as home to Detachment G, the Agency's mobile worldwide deployment capability, up to the phase-out of its U-2 operations in 1974. Following the May Day 1960 shoot down, the personnel and equipment withdrawn from Det B at Adana and Det C at Astugi were consolidated at Edwards AFB, under cover of WRSP-IV by September 1960. Detachment G's role took it to operating locations around the world. Sometimes for short periods and at others for intermittent commitments extending over several years. It sometimes had to move between widely separated locations across the world at very short notice. As the US became embroiled in North Vietnam, Cambodia and Laos, CIA operated U-2s flew missions across all three. There were overflights of Tibet, China and along the Sino-Indian border.

Polecat

Five of Det G's most experienced U-2 pilots arrived at NAS Cubi Point in the Philippines from Edwards in January 1961. Jim Baker, Jim Cherbonneaux, Al Rand, EK Jones and Buster Edens, deployed there with two aircraft (Art 343 and 344). Colonel William Gregory had not long been appointed Det G commander and this was his first overseas deployment. He and his staff put together the 'Go hit' for the mission, containing all the items they thought necessary. This was transported by C-124 and a KC-135A, which doubled as a recovery aircraft, in case a U-2 diverted elsewhere during a mission. Operation Polecat was a series of seven flights (3018 to 3026, excluding 3021 and 3023) ordered by Eisenhower. His administration was concerned that the Laotian government could collapse, possibly leading to a North Vietnamese or Chinese invasion.[1] The missions looked for signs of insurgent and military activities along the North Vietnamese and Laotian border; ultimately they revealed no suspicious activity.[2] Mission 3018 flown, by Jim Baker on 3 January 1961, covered southern Hainan Island on his way in and along the joint border. It contrailed heavily at an unusually high altitude, which might have given away Baker's presence, had it not been for the heavy cloud and haze; it also prevented good photography.[3]

The next day's mission (3019) pushed further north. The fuel load was reduced in an attempt to ease contrailing, but it did not work. Fortunately, it was masked again by heavy cloud, but when Cherbonneaux saw the weather ahead clearing, he decided to abort the mission rather than give away his presence.[4] A further reduced fuel load seemed to do the trick for 3020 on 5 January, piloted by Al Rand, in Art 344. He collected imagery over the Laotian border areas and parts of Vietnam. The next four missions were similarly successful, some affected by cloud, overflying all of North Vietnam and Laos. Airfields, major army bases and a few naval installations comprised the majority of the targets imaged. Unusually the ELINT report for Mission 3025 has made it into the archive. It details the presence of Chinese SCR-270, SCR-588 plus 'Knife Rest' A and B radars, along its flight route. The report even describes the points from when and where the radars were able to track Art 344 as it passed them. The details were considered confirmatory, as the presence of all four radars was already well known.[5]

The photographic 'take' and ELINT tapes from each Polecat mission were transported by C-130 to Yakota AB, for onward movement to the US for full processing. Material from two earlier Polecat missions had been processed by Eastman Kodak at Rochester and was being sent by an Agency operated C-47, to Bolling AFB for NPIC in Washington DC on 14 March 1961. During the flight, an engine failed and to lighten the load the crew threw out the 43 boxes of U-2 film over a rugged area near Williamsport, Pennsylvania. After successfully making an emergency landing at a nearby airfield, the state police were asked to seal off the area. Ten Agency security staff quickly went to the now cordoned area and successfully recovered all 43 boxes.[6]

Art 358 and Al Rand returned to Cubi Point for a single mission (3055) on 15 August 1961. He flew a coastal route northwards, along the Vietnamese coast, until reaching Hanoi, when he tracked inland, flew around the Chinese border area before he headed outbound over Hanoi again, then over the sea back towards Cubi Point. He passed the western side of Hainan and over the Paracel Islands, one of many similar missions over the next eight years.

Low Note

Early the following year Bob Ericson flew four missions from Taoyuan, between 21 February 1962 (3066) and 7 April 1962 (Mission 3076). Primarily targeted against North Vietnam, the 'Low Note' overflights departed Taoyuan, crossed the Vietnamese coast, following it northwards. 3076 maintained a high-altitude circuit around the very north of the country, before photographing the South Vietnamese-Laotian border area, as it headed south again. The first, Mission 3066, on 21 February 1962, additionally imaged the southern half of Hainan, as the flight skirted the island's western and southern coasts, as it returned to Taoyuan. The still heavily redacted mission warning order contains a detailed Vietnamese air ORBAT, with precise locations for 20 air defence radars. These radars were attributed as having done an: 'excellent job of tracking aircraft in the past. It is an extension of the Chicom air defence network'.

Attempting to keep the Chinese and Vietnamese air defences guessing, the last Low Note flight, Mission 3076, was the most ambitious. Piloted by Bob Ericson in Art 378, it covered the north coast of Hainan on the outward leg, the southern coast on its return and a large number of targets in the Chinese border area, Vietnam and Laos.[7] There were three further flights (6056, 6058 and 6060) in May, June and July 1962 that followed the same mission pattern as the Low Note sorties, although they kept clear of Hainan.[8] Subsequently, there were no significant Det G Asian missions until December 1962, after the climax of the Cuban missile crisis.

Air Refuelling

The CIA enhanced the U-2's range by installing aerial refuelling equipment, but the type's unique, glider like design posed significant challenges. Det G was at the heart of this activity, both at Edwards and in its later operational employment.

Whilst the U-2 had considerable range, an ability to air refuel brought even the most inaccessible targets potentially within range. The conversions were completed for both CIA and SAC aircraft from standard C models and gave the aircraft an endurance of over 10 hours.[9] As a result, the pilot's oxygen supply became the limiting factor, later solved by the installation of an additional oxygen bottle. Art 342 was the trials aircraft, the refuelling receptacle fitted in a short spine fairing aft of the Q-bay cover.

The fragility and speed of the U-2 were always issues for aerial refuelling operations. At the refuelling speed of 200kts, this was at the low end of the KC-135's performance envelope. The join up technique was also unusual. The U-2 flew straight and level (around 35,000ft) and the KC-135A overtook it, passing down the left-hand side, slightly above it. About a quarter of a mile past the U-2, the

The CIA's U-2Fs and SAC's U-2Es could air refuel from KC-135A Stratotankers. The refuelling receptacle was installed in a fuselage 'hump' fairing. It also housed guide lights for night refuelling, a Collins 618-T3 single-sideband radio for secure communication, with an approximate 3,000-mile range, plus a rendezvous beacon and antenna. (CIA)

Refuelling the U-2F was a delicate affair, because of the U-2's slow speed and its vulnerability if caught by the KC-135's jet engine exhaust. (CIA)

moved to the side and began climbing to his operational altitude. He had to keep well clear of the KC-135's engine vortices. On 1 March 1962 Captain John Campbell died during a night refuelling. His U-2 flipped over in the jet wash and he was unable to escape. Agency pilot John Hall was luckier on 25 February 1966, when Art 342 was lost on a training flight. Hall had carried out nine successful dry hook-ups. The final one was an emergency breakaway which worked well. After that, he positioned himself alongside the tanker and initiated a standard break away. In what appeared to be a normal manoeuvre, there may have been a fuel leak from the trailing edge of the left wing-root, then the U-2's left wing broke off. The wing fell away but the U-2's engine flashed past, close to the tanker. Fortunately, Hall successfully

tanker slowed slightly. The U-2 gently climbed into position, behind the now lowered refuelling boom. The boom was flown into the receptacle by the operator on board the KC-135. Once refuelled the U-2 pilot eased power back slightly, disconnected, dropped 100ft, baled out, whilst the KC-135A circled the incident site until relieved by SAR helicopters.[10]

Takhli Air Base

For the 1959–1960 Det C overflights, Takhli had been just a makeshift staging base. However, it was developed to become a much more permanent facility, for Dets G, H and soon the US Air Force U-2s. From there a wider range of alternative routes was possible, much more of South East Asia came within range. Takhli provided different access routes into China, particularly through the western part of the country, important for extremely long-range missions to the north. Tibet, occupied by Chinese forces since 1960, came within range too. Missions were soon regularly mounted from Thailand against North Vietnam, Cambodia and Laos, interspersed with overflights of Tibet and Kashmir. So began a series of 24 missions that were flown from the Thai airbase from December 1962 to December 1963.

Indian Gateway

The U-2F's aerial refuelling capability was first employed operationally on missions over the Sino-Indian border area and Tibet, in December 1962 and January 1963.[11] Following border clashes between the two, the Indian government asked for US assistance. The Americans also sought hard intelligence from the area. The Indians permitted the U-2 overflights to transit and refuel in their airspace, flying from Takhli via the Indian Ocean. Prime Minister Nehru and the Indian authorities granted emergency diversion permission for any mission that experienced in-flight difficulties.

Art 342, with a support team, deployed to Takhli and Mission 3201 was launched on 5 December 1962, flown by Al Rand. A C-130 supplied logistic support whilst an SA-16 Albatross 10071 c/s Gem 87, with a six-man crew, provided rescue cover. In addition to its mission crew, the KC-135A carried an eight-man U-2 recovery team, in case a diversion was necessary. The SA-16 carried paratroopers, trained to rescue the U-2 pilots if they went down over land or water.[12] Refuelling was carried out on the return flight leg after the U-2 had re-entered Indian airspace and had to be completed quickly, or it would have needed to make an emergency fuel diversion. Flying over the Himalayas, wind speeds were consistently higher than predicted, which adversely impacted fuel consumption rates. Despite the 140kt wind across the refuelling track, the fuel transfer was 'very professionally' accomplished by KC-135A 57-2601 (c/s Mate 32). It took much longer than expected because fuel icing restricted the booms' rate of fuel flow. This was resolved on later missions with a simple fuel additive. Rand's mission was airborne for a stunning 11 hours 45 minutes.

By Mission 3203, the whole process, from joining to break away, was completed in less than five minutes, as the U-2 only required a very small fuel offload. The missions were regarded as successful, but most experienced significant turbulence and extensive cloud cover, which reduced the amount of useable imagery collected.

In a Top Secret message, the mission commander subsequently wrote:

These Missions are the most difficult we have ever attempted, with regards to the amount of required preparation and actual execution, due to the inordinate amount of extra effort required. This is necessitated by lengthy missions, numbers of aircraft, and flight plans to be briefed and coordinated and the extra amount of coordination required with other stations.[13]

Whilst aerial refuelling gave range advantages, it created significantly longer sortie times, seriously exhausting the pilots. On occasion, two U-2 missions took place simultaneously. This was done sometimes to catch snapshots of a wider area at the same time and confuse hostile air defences. This was the plan for Mission 3206 from Takhli, which was to fly over North Vietnam and GRC135 from Taoyuan, to cover western China, close to the North Vietnamese border on 27 December 1962. In their briefings, both pilots were told they were likely to pass within eight nautical miles of each other, on respective sides of the border at the same time.[14] However, GRC135 aborted soon after take-off, when its System XII malfunctioned, the mission instead flown the next day, as GRC136.[15] Mission 3206 was the first Det G flight from Takhli, after the Cuban missile crisis. It crossed into Chinese airspace, and completed substantial coverage of North Vietnam, before it returned to Takhli, mirroring the Laos border but outside of its airspace.[16]

For Mission 3213, the U-2's c/s was 'Hot Dog', but in an emergency would have used the c/s 'Red Fox', to indicate it was experiencing problems, whilst KC-135A (57-1441) carried a recovery crew.[17] On 22 January 1963, Edens' Mission 3215, suffered a depressurisation in the Q-bay. As a result, the bay heater burned out, but in doing so the camera hatch cover warped which allowed light to leak into the bay and damaged some of the film.[18] For this series of flights, between January and May, even these very experienced pilots reported that navigation could be especially difficult. The relatively featureless mountainous terrain made it difficult to accurately determine their position. Their combined imagery showed a relatively settled military situation, mostly identifying military areas, convoys, barracks and a few airfields.

Another sustained batch of 14 missions was launched from Takhli, between 1 March 1963 and 17 November, primarily targeted against North Vietnam, Laos, Burma and Chinese border areas. These missions illustrated the deepening American involvement in the South East Asian theatre. Their coverage was also becoming more tactical than strategic, as the US ground presence ramped up. Large amounts of that imagery were quickly downgraded in classification terms, taken outside the Top Secret codeword structure generally used for U-2 intelligence, so it could be more easily shared with the US military.

Irregularly numbered Mission 6066 was flown on 11 August 1963 by Marty Knutson, from Takhli. He mainly covered targets over North Vietnam, some 11 airfields including some in the Hanoi area. He also overflew Hainan Island and Sanya airfield in the extreme south, probably on his return leg to Taoyuan.[19]

Interspersed with these missions over Vietnam, between September and November 1963 were four more (3227, 3230, 3236 and 3238), aimed at Tibet and China from Takhli.[20] The missions went ahead as planned, but last-minute cancellation was always a real possibility, with the final go-ahead only arriving at the very last moment. Bad weather, changed routes and equipment failures were all quite common reasons for cancellations. Equally frequent were political and administrative cancellations, but they are rarely recorded. Mission 3236, an overflight due to cover Bhutan, Sikkim and Nepal, is one of those rarely documented examples. Just one hour 40 minutes before Al Rand's planned take-off, at 1400 hours, James Cunningham, the Acting Assistant Director for Special Activities, was informally told that just two hours earlier COMOR had decided it no longer required the mission. That Committee determined target requirements and priorities. Now unsure about sending the final mission 'Go' message to Takhli, he frantically sought clarification. Having been assured that the CIA Director still required the mission to go ahead, he finally passed the 'Go' message 40 minutes late, less than 50 minutes before its scheduled launch. Sometimes the final

'Go' was delayed even further and would not be received until after the planned departure time. If delays were significant, they adversely affected the quality of photographic imagery and ELINT data collected over the target area. Nevertheless, on that day the SAR SA-16 Albatross and KC-135A launched on time as did Al Rand. Cloud cover affected only the final part of his mission. On his return leg, the tanker hook-up was accomplished without incident. Rand's flight was airborne for 12 hours 25 minutes. The preliminary report after the flight revealed that there was very little military activity in Tibet, the most obvious being continued road- and bridge-building, with the presence of tented construction camps.[21] A 10 November 1963 (3238) mission, along the Sino-Burmese and Sino-Indian border, was followed by three flights between 14 and 17 November 1963. These were over border areas of Vietnam, Burma and Laos conducted at the request of Thailand's prime minister.[22]

South America

Det G's return to Edwards AFB was only brief. Between 3 and 19 December 1963, it was deployed to Ramey AFB in Puerto Rico. From there Jim Barnes, Bob Ericson and Buster Edens undertook a series of six photographic sorties (3250 to 3257, excluding 3251 and 3255), flying two missions each. The flights were principally directed at Venezuela, where its democratic government was fragile and there were fears it might fall under Cuban influence or control. The overflights looked for evidence of guerrilla and 'anti-government' activity. Two missions covered Venezuela using a coastal and interior search pattern. Two more targeted neighbouring British Guiana, one flying an interior route, with the final two undertaking coverage of both countries. Guiana was experiencing its own internal political strife, a source of concern for the British and Americans, worried about the activities of nationalist party leader Cheddi Jagan. Agency records indicate the British were kept in the dark about the overflights of their colony.[23]

South East Asia Operations Ramp-up

Just ten days after returning from Ramey AFB, Det G was again in action from Takhli. From 29 December 1963 to the end of April 1964 coverage

of South East Asia stepped up considerably, with some 20 missions covering North Vietnam, Laos and Cambodia. Mission 6070 (29 December 1963) was flown by Al Rand, and 6071 by Jim Bedford the following day. This was the operational debut of the new 112A camera (see Chapter 6) in South East Asia, adapted from the KH-3 Corona reconnaissance satellites. It used a 24-inch f3.5 'Petzval' design lens, to obtain stereo photography. From 70,000ft it covered a 16.5nm-wide strip, by one mile deep. It produced particularly high-quality, stereographic imagery of directly overflown targets. It had a smaller width of coverage than the B camera but achieved even better resolution. The purpose of the missions was described as being intended to provide 'baseline photography of the border area' between South Vietnam and its Cambodian and Laotian neighbours. The mission IPIRs show extensive coverage of Laos. A final mission of the series was added on 7 January 1964, (0014E),

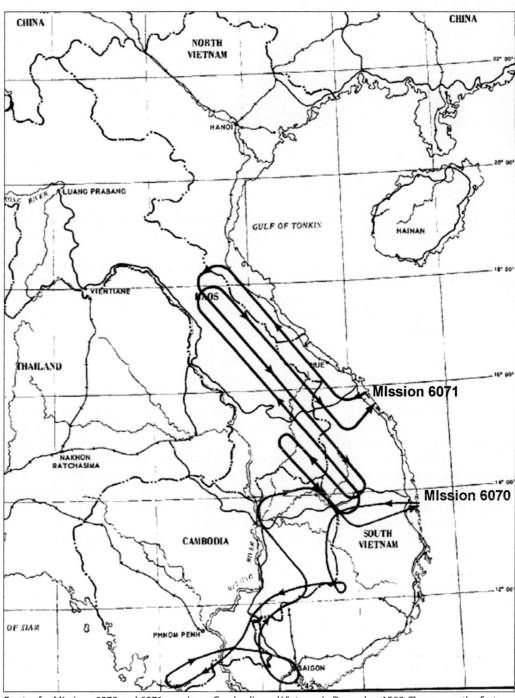

Routes for Missions 6070 and 6071 over Laos, Cambodia and Vietnam in December 1963. These were the first operational use of the new 112B camera. (CIA)

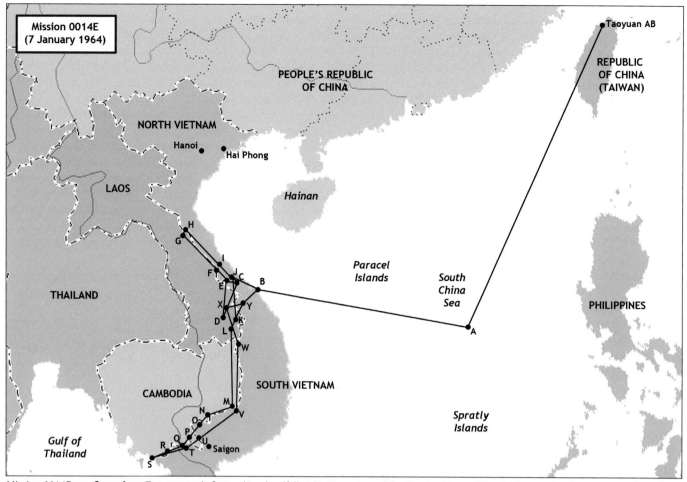

Mission 0014E was flown from Taoyuan and after making landfall at Da Nang, traced the Cambodian and South Vietnam border areas searching for evidence of insurgents. (Map by Tom Cooper based on Data SIO, NOAA, USN, NGA, GEBCO and Landsat/Copernicus)

flown by Al Rand, from Taoyuan, using the 112A camera to search again for military concentrations and possible infiltration points.

A 45-day TDY period to the region saw four extensive overflights of the area in spring 1964. The first was on 23 February 1964 (0034E), the second (0064E) on 28 February, with S074E on 1 March and S104E on 6 March 1964. The first covered a search pattern, flying north-east to south-east return legs, across the whole of South Vietnam and over part of the Cambodian border area. The second flight was much wider-ranging, reaching across Laos and as far north as the Chinese border area. S074E again covered targets across Laos and Vietnam, while the final one, S104E, concentrated on overflying central Laos from south to north.

In February 1964, USAF U-2s were unceremoniously ordered out by the Philippines government, unhappy about the launching of its 'Lucky Dragon' code-named missions against Vietnam. In March, Agency U-2s were allocated responsibility for covering North Vietnam, Cambodia and Laos. SAC was made responsible for coverage of South Vietnam, a decision that paved the way for USAF U-2 operations from Bien Hoa.

From 11 March to 15 April 1964 CIA pilots flew a group of 14 missions from Takhli, giving blanket coverage of the region. The missions were again flown by some of the most experienced pilots: Marty Knutson, Bob Ericson and Buster Edens. T124A flown by Edens on 31 March, entered PRC airspace from Laos and concentrated its coverage on western China into Tibet. The return leg largely mirrored the Indian and Burmese border.[24] The missions amounted to a final surge of Detachment G operations from Takhli, thereafter missions in-theatre flown by Agency pilots were few and far between.

One further flight, Mission S214A was a single high priority flight request. Flown by Al Rand, in Art 342, from Cubi Point on 24 April 1964. His two main targets appear to be longitude and latitude coordinates in the middle of the North Vietnamese countryside, not far from the Laotian border. They are simply recorded as 'special target coverage'.[25]

Charbatia

Missions over Tibet became more sustainable when Charbatia AB in India, was identified as a potential long-term U-2 operating location. The Indian government agreed to make the airfield available and improvement work began to make it suitable for detachment-size operations. After considerable delays, it was finally ready from 1 May 1964, with supplies and equipment airlifted in by USAF C-124s. T284A was the first of several planned missions over a seven-day period, agreed with the Indian government. Launched on 24 May 1964, flown by Bob Ericson, his overflight took him beyond Lhasa, but only two airfields were detected. The military presence around the Tibetan capital consisted of just a few barracks, some small, isolated facilities elsewhere and construction units. On returning to Charbatia Art 342's brakes failed. As Ericson attempted to slow the aircraft by dragging the wingtips, it ran off the edge of the runway at around 20 to 30kts. The nose wheel sank 14 to 16 inches into the earth and struck a submerged rock, folding the front landing gear back nearly flush with the fuselage. There was also damage to the drift sight, lower fuselage, aileron skin and wheel-well, and it caused minor fuel leaks. It also broke the tracker camera lens. However, the damage was said to be less than if he had gone off the end of the runway where there were large piles of bricks and half-buried

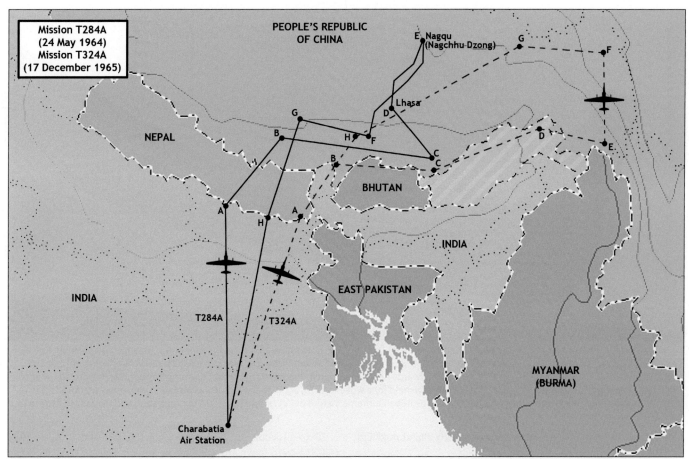

Charbatia AB in India was a valuable location for launching missions over the Himalayas to Tibet. T284A was a single mission on 24 May 1964 with T324A on 17 December 1964, part of a three-flight group covering broadly similar routes. (Map by Tom Cooper based on Landsat/Copernicus, Data SIO, USN, NGA and GEBCO)

stones. Insult was added to injury because only one airbag was available to lift the aircraft, so it had to stay near the end of the runway covered in canvas and under guard until a C-130 brought more airbags to lift Art 342 and place it on a dolly.

The undamaged mission film was later airlifted out and said to be of high quality. Art 342 was disassembled and removed in a C-124.[26] In Beijing's press and radio news on 25 May 1964, there were announcements that an Indian aircraft had penetrated PRC airspace. They gave near accurate location sequences and times for T284A's flight. This led Agency officials to believe Ericson probably contrailed at times, as there were only brief detections of Chinese radar activity.[27] As there were no replacement U-2s readily available and Prime Minister Nehru died

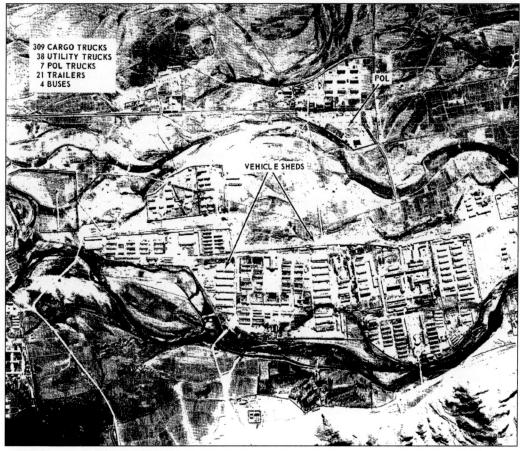

One of the few significant subjects revealed by T344A were Chinese Barracks at Norbu Lingka, then on the outskirts of Lhasa. (CIA)

Art 359/56-6692 probably had one of the most varied careers in U-2 history. It is now suspended from the roof of the American Air Museum Hall at Duxford IWM. It served as a U-2A, U-2C, was converted to a U-2F and flew with SAC against Cuba. From Charbatia it made overflights of Tibet and China. From 1971 it was used as a project test aircraft at Edwards AFB. It took part in the development programme for the USAF Advanced Location Strike System programme, where it deployed to RAF Wethersfield for a while in 1975. Soon afterwards it was modified into a two-seat U-2CT and in early 1988 was retired to RAF Alconbury as a Battle Damage Repair airframe, before being returned to U-2A configuration and moved to Duxford in 1992. (Kevin Wright)

suddenly on 27 May 1964, the operation was quietly abandoned and the Americans withdrew.

They returned in December 1964 for three more border reconnaissance missions. Good weather allowed comprehensive coverage of the entire area with Art 359 by pilots Marty Knutson, Al Baker and Dan Schmarr. T314A on 16 December was followed by T324A the following day and T344A on 20 December. The missions largely confirmed the area empty of significant military forces, although some troops were being employed on continued infrastructure construction.

The US wanted its use of Charbatia to grow. It would have provided much better access to Lop Nor and the nuclear testing sites and met the joint US–Indian requirement to monitor Chinese activities in Tibet and along the Sino-Indian border. However, those intentions never matured and any possibility of a TACKLE-like operation with the Indians was rejected by the Office of Special Activities (OSA). By July 1967 most of the equipment had been airlifted out, much of it sent to Takhli where operations were scaling up.[28]

Det G Overflights Wind Down

Two further missions were flown over Cambodia by Agency pilots from Takhli. The first, on 29 October 1965 (S015A), by Dan Schmarr followed by Jim Barnes (S025A) on 7 November 1965. Little detailed information is available on either. Barnes entered Cambodian airspace from Thailand, flying east to west along much of the Thai-Cambodian border. He then covered most of the rest of the country by following the Cambodian coast returning to Takhli.[30]

Mission 0026H was flown on 3 February 1966 and covered the Vietnamese-Laotian border, passed down into Cambodia before looping back heading northwards along the Vietnamese coast, imaging with its 112B camera.[31]

Two missions on 27 March 1968 (S018E) and 3 April 1968 (S028E) were flown from Takhli by Robert Hall in Art 385. They were the first Det G Far East operational missions for over two years and would also be their last. They followed the Cambodian-Thai border from around 30km inside Cambodia, starting near the tri-border area between Cambodia, Thailand and Laos. The first lasted four hours and the second five hours, covering nearly 1,400nm and 1,600nm respectively. On S018E the Delta III camera imaged Samrong airfield and some road construction. The post-mission reports indicated 'no significant military intelligence' was revealed by the flights.[32]

It is this period of operations from the early to mid-1960s, that is probably the most complex in the U-2's history, with Detachments G and H operating alongside each other at the same time. Detachment H was mounting missions over China from Taoyuan and to a lesser extent Takhli. As Agency resources became stretched, TACKLE pilots increasingly took on flights, covering parts of North Korea from Taoyuan and some staging operations out of Kunsan, in South Korea. Towards the end of the 1960s, TACKLE missions switched to being peripheral only operations, along the PRC coast.

In 1969, Det G changed its unclassified cover from being WRSP-IV to become the 1130th Air Technical Training Group, later changed again to become the 1130th Aerospace Technical Development and Training Group (ATTG), taking on responsibility for SR-71 crews, as well as the gradually contracting U-2 programme. In addition to its operational commitments, Detachment G still had major responsibility for the development and testing of new equipment and capabilities. One of the most astounding was enabling selected U-2 airframes to operate from US aircraft carriers.

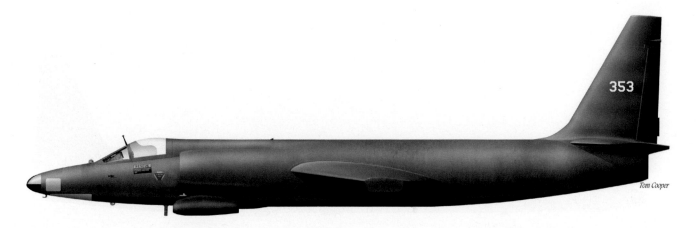

Even once the USAF assumed responsibility for high-altitude radioactive sampling operations, the CIA retained the capability to run covert flights using a specialised pod and equipment fitted into the Q-bay of its U-2s. This U-2A (Article 353) is shown as equipped with the HASP intake: this was installed on the hatch cover, on the left side of the Q-bay. The jet is shown as still wearing the semi-gloss version of the USN's Sea Blue (originally designated AN607 non-specular sea blue, later FS25042, and then, in its matt version, FS35042), as applied fleet-wide starting in 1959. (Artwork by Tom Cooper)

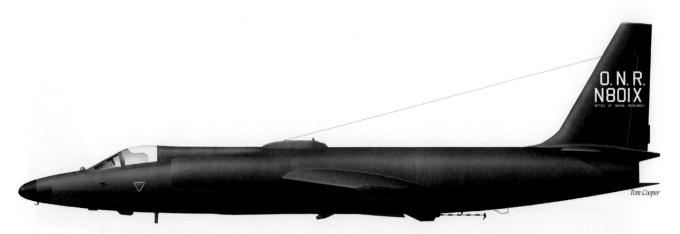

Still wearing the non-specular sea blue, but already equipped with an arrestor hook, and disingenuously marked as 'N801X' from the 'Office of Naval Research', this U-2G (Article 348) was deployed for carrier trials- and pilot-qualification purposes in March 1964. The nose skid is shown as in the closed position, while clearly visible are the deflector and arrestor hook installation under the centre of the lower fuselage. (Artwork by Tom Cooper)

Starting in 1965, U-2s were gradually re-painted in matt black colour known as 'black velvet', developed to reduce their radar echo. It was in this colour that this U-2F entered service with the 35th 'Black Cat' Squadron, Republic of China Air Force. Notably, the aircraft was equipped with in-flight refuelling capability, which proved vital for the long-range missions over Tibet and Cuba. The refuelling receptacle and associated guide lights were all installed within the front section of the elongated Collins 'radio hump', atop of the fuselage. (Artwork by Tom Cooper)

In November 1969, Lockheed pilot Bill Park deployed to the aircraft carrier USS *America* (CVA-66) with the U-2R 'Article 055', to prove the new variant's suitability for carrier operations. Like the U-2G before, the aircraft was equipped with a (removable) arrestor tail-hook: new additions included wingtip skids, a strengthened landing gear, and foldable outer wing sections. By the time of U-2R's service entry, the 'black velvet' overall livery was in fleet-wide use. (Artwork by Tom Cooper)

The Taiwanese Detachment H flew U-2Rs from Taoyuan Air Base. For missions off the mainland People's Republic of China, flown from May 1968 to May 1974, its aircraft were usually equipped wither with the 'Long Shaft' SIGINT system or the new 'H' camera. All the U-2Rs operated by the ROCAF wore a bare minimum of any kind of markings: indeed, these were limited to a four-digit serial in red on the fin, and a small national marking on the rear fuselage. Inset is shown the insignia of the 35th 'Black Cat' Squadron. (Artwork by Tom Cooper)

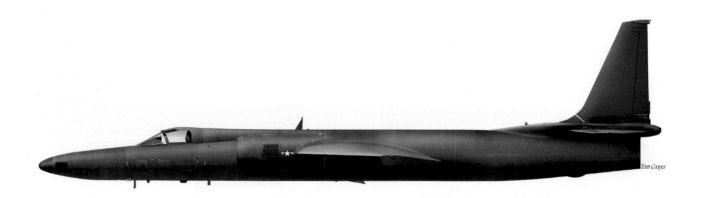

When the Detachment G deployed its U-2Rs to the United Kingdom – for periodic missions within Operation Scope Saint, from late 1960s onwards – the British requested them to carry the standard 'Star and Bar' insignia national markings of the US Air Force. This was applied in rather small size, on the intakes, directly in front of the wing's leading edge. (Artwork by Tom Cooper)

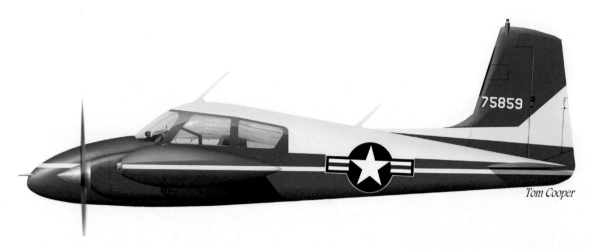

The CIA often deployed Cessna U-3As – all still wearing their USAF markings (including the service title, U. S. Air Force, applied in white on the side of the cabin, not visible here) – to support U-2 detachments, as chase aircraft, for local communication duties, and as emergency evacuation aircraft. (Artwork by Tom Cooper)

Lockheed C-130As (shown here is the example with FY-serial number 56-0532 from the 322nd Air Division) were deployed to transport equipment for Operation Fast Move – the deployment exercise to RAF Watton, in October 1959. Many other C-130s of the USAF regularly flew in support of the Agency's U-2 operations, ferrying equipment – and sometimes transporting exposed mission films – as and when necessary. For most of the 1950s and well into the 1960s, the entire fleet was operated in bare metal overall livery, with most of the fin and parts of the rear fuselage in day-glo orange. (Artwork by Tom Cooper)

Lockheed C-141A Starlifters took over many of the support tasks for the larger U-2Rs from the C-124s, as the latter was gradually phased out of service. Their large cargo hold could carry more equipment over longer distances and faster than the C-130s. In the event of a serious fault developing during forward-based operations, the U-2R could be disassembled, mounted on specially designed dolly racks and evacuated by C-141As. Early during their service, all the Starlifters were left in bare metal, with only their fins and rear fuselage painted in light blue-grey. (Artwork by Tom Cooper)

The roomier cockpit of the U-2R enabled the pilots to wear the David Clark S1010 Full Pressure Suit (and later the S1031, similar to the S1030 worn by the crews of the Lockheed SR-71). This was a great improvement for crew comfort in comparison to the earlier Partial Pressure Suit. (Artwork by Anderson Subtil)

The improved B2 version of the legendary B camera became available from 1966 and could produce even better quality imagery. It was slightly smaller, weighed nearly 100lbs less, had improved optics, smoother internal film movement mechanisms and was more reliable. (CIA)

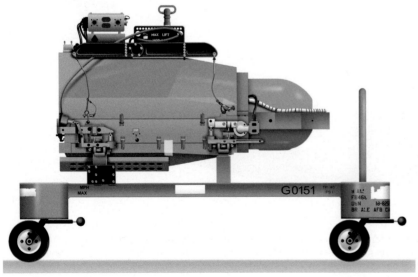

The ITEK-produced KA-80 camera, often better known as the Optical Bar Camera (OBC) became available from late 1968. Originally 13 were purchased (six each for the CIA and USAF, plus a spare), and was also used by the SR-71A Blackbird. Because of the high quality of the images it produces, in recent years it has sometimes been used by USAF U-2s to collect imagery of major disaster areas to assist rescue and recovery agencies. (Artwork by Anderson Subtil)

The U-2G marked as N812X, as seen about to launch from USS *America*. (CIA)

A line-up of the first batch of U-2Rs, seen at Edwards North Air Force Base. Visible in the foreground is the prototype U-2R, N803X (Article 061, FY-serial 68-10329). (CIA)

In March 1971 U-2R Art 051 (68-10329) arrived in Taiwan to join Det H, flying many peripheral missions. Passed to the USAF in 1974, seen here at RAF Fairford in 2004, now a U-2S, being towed with its pogos fitted backwards. (Kevin Slade)

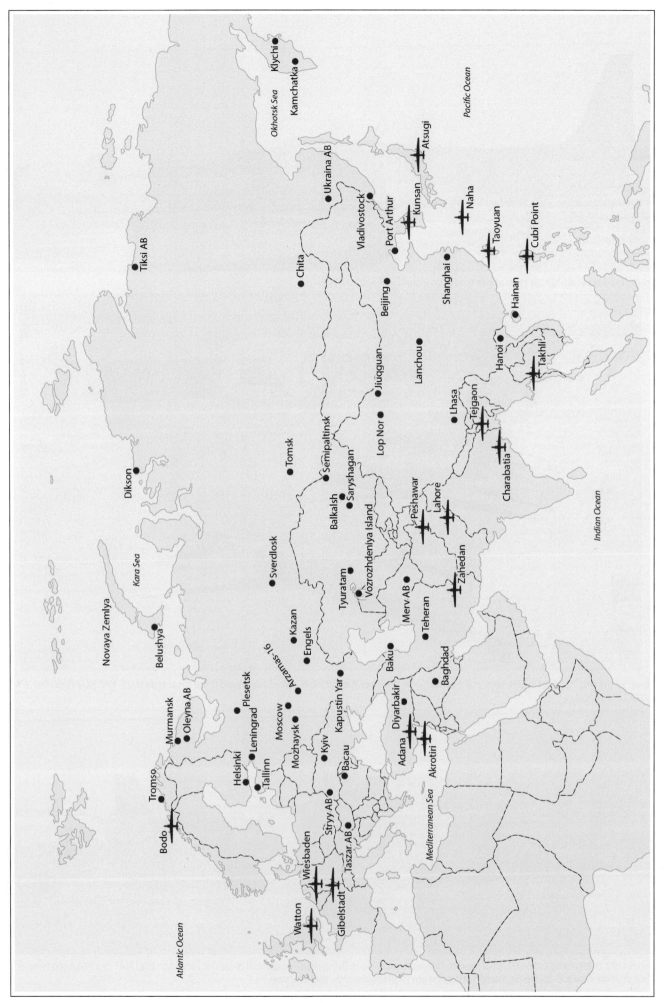

This map shows airfields from which CIA U-2 operations took place and other key locations described in this book. (Map by George Anderson)

Table 3: U-2 Fleet at 25 October 1965[29]

Art	Model	User	Air Refuel	Systems						Slipper Tanks	Drop Tanks	Bird Watcher
				III	IV	VI	IXB	XIIB	XIIIA			
342	F	CIA	✓	✓		✓	✓	✓		✓		✓
347	E	SAC	✓	✓	✓							
348	G	CIA		✓		✓	✓	✓	✓	✓		✓
349	H	CIA	✓	✓		✓	✓	✓	✓	✓	✓	✓
359	F	CIA	✓	✓		✓	✓	✓	✓	✓		✓
363	A	SAC		✓								
367	A	SAC		✓						✓		
368	Spec	AFSC										
372	F	CIA	✓	✓		✓	✓	✓	✓	✓		✓
373	A	SAC		✓								
374	E	SAC	✓	✓	✓							
375	A	SAC		✓								
381	G	CIA		✓		✓				✓		✓
383	C	CIA		✓		✓				✓		✓
384	C	CIA		✓		✓	✓	✓	✓	✓		✓
385	G	CIA				✓	✓	✓	✓	✓		✓
386	A	SAC		✓	✓							
388	D	AFSC										
389	A	AFSC										
390	A	SAC		✓								
391	A	SAC		✓								
392	A	SAC		✓								
393	A	SAC		✓								
394	D	AFSC										

By 25 October 1965, the complete U-2 fleet was down to just 24 aircraft of an original combined CIA/USAF purchase of 55 airframes. It illustrates how the CIA airframes were much more comprehensively equipped with SIGINT collection and self-defence equipment, than the SACs U2A/Es. By then Air Force Systems Command used dedicated U-2s as test aircraft.

5

THE U-2 GOES TO SEA

In the early years the CIA was not very receptive to US Navy suggestions for carrier-based U-2 operations; however, after the loss of Gary Powers attitudes began to change. As U-2 overseas basing possibilities contracted, the prospect of carrier-based operations looked more attractive and offered the potential to reach otherwise inaccessible targets. Kelly Johnson was approached to suggest the necessary modifications. His proposals included strengthening the rear fuselage and landing gear, fitting an arrestor hook and installing a fuel dump mechanism. Probably most important was the fitting of wing spoilers, intended to quickly unload wing lift on touchdown and activated by a cockpit switch.[1] More complex modifications proposals included installing retractable pogos, fitting JATO pods, making detachable wingtips and a significantly redesigned landing gear.

The Agency selected the more minimal option. Discussions with the Navy identified the likely optimal ways in which the carrier could be manoeuvred and positioned to optimise U-2 operations.

Organised under the unclassified codename 'Whale Tale' it was divided into three phases. The first involved Lockheed's testing of the new U-2G as the variant was designated, to ensure it was suitable and prepared for going to sea.[2] Phase two was the training of company and Agency pilots for carrier operations in the modified aircraft. The final phase was the deployment of a combined group of Lockheed, Agency HQ and Det G personnel onto a carrier.

It was recognised that handling the U-2 once it was on the carrier would be a major challenge. Taking it below deck required using one of the side-mounted aircraft lifts. Given the U-2's wingspan, it meant one wing would hang out over the sea. To move the U-2 towards the lift a 'lowboy' wheeled trolley was designed to be placed under the fuselage and allow it to be castored around the deck into the required position. When using the lift, given the propensity for the aircraft to tip towards the heaviest wing, it was essential that the inboard wing tip rested on the lift, appropriately weighted to ensure the U-2 did not topple off into the sea.

U-2G below deck on USS *Ranger*, winched aboard by crane. (CIA)

N808X Carrier touchdown on 29 February 1964. Modifications included fitting tail hook and nose 'bumper' in case the aircraft nosed down on deck after catching a wire. (CIA)

By the time N801X arrived on USS *Ranger* on 2 March, the nose underside was fitted with a spring-loaded pogo, felt to be more resilient than the original nose bumper. (CIA)

After trials at Edwards AFB, the first test was of a U-2C at sea in August 1963. This was essentially a Lockheed operation using an unmodified aircraft for a simple take-off test. After flying to NAS North Island, San Diego, the aircraft was emptied of fuel and winched aboard USS *Kitty Hawk*, using a specially designed sling, and then hidden below deck on the night of 2 August. The cover story for carrier operations was to be that the aircraft was undertaking tasks for the Office of Naval Research and hence the large ONR title applied to its tail. On 3 August, steaming off the coast, U-2C Art 352 (marked N315X) with Lockheed pilot Bob Schumacher, successfully

On the rear undercarriage doors, small deflectors were fitted to ensure a bouncing deck cable did not snag the wheels. (CIA)

N315X being moved above deck on USS *Ranger* using the specially designed dolly, before Bill Park performed the first U-2 carrier take-off. (CIA)

launched. It took off using only a third of the available distance on *Kitty Hawk*'s deck and climbed steeply away. It returned to enter the carrier's circuit, performed approaches and a touch-and-go before it headed to shore.

Following that test, the next stage was a full deployment aboard USS *Ranger*. The selected pilots underwent preparatory training, planned in groups of four. From November 1963, this involved quick conversion to the T-2A Buckeye, with carrier landing practice at NAS Pensacola and deck qualification onto USS *Lexington* in the Gulf of Mexico. The final element involved returning to Edwards to practise the same procedures in a U-2G using a specially constructed area, under the guidance of an experienced Navy Landing Signals Officer, until he was satisfied with their competence to approach and land on board a carrier. The final phase of training started in February 1964 with the arrival of the first U-2G conversion at Edwards AFB.

On 29 February, USS *Ranger* set sail for a test area off San Diego. Lockheed pilot Bob Schumacher in Art 362 (marked as N808X) flew a touch-and-go across its deck. However, on landing he bounced, his hook engaged the lightweight cable and unceremoniously dumped his U-2 nose down on the deck. Fortunately, the damage was relatively minor and after some quick work Schumacher took off, headed for Burbank and a better repair. On 2 March

Schumacher returned in a different aircraft (Art 348 marked as N801X) and completed four successful arrested landings. On the same day, Bob Ericson began his qualification flights and took off from *Ranger* in Art 348. He carried out approaches and touch-and-goes but abandoned his arrested landings as he was running low on fuel. With other ships in sight of the carrier, he returned to land, and arrived with only five gallons left in his fuel tank! On 3 March, Jim Barnes flew Art 348 back to the carrier. As he landed wing low on *Ranger*'s deck he slightly damaged the wingtip and skid on the arrestor wire but managed to get airborne again and headed back to Edwards AFB. USS *Ranger* headed back to NAS North Island. The training was recommenced on 9 and 10 March with the necessary repairs completed. Bedford damaged the nose of his aircraft on his third trap attempt on 10 March in a similar manner to the first incident. This time it was repaired below deck by the Lockheed engineers on the ship. Barnes and Schumacher took the two aircraft back to Edwards AFB. Bedford, Barnes, Edens and RAF Squadron Leader Ivan Webster had all completed their four traps on the ship, gaining their carrier qualification.[3]

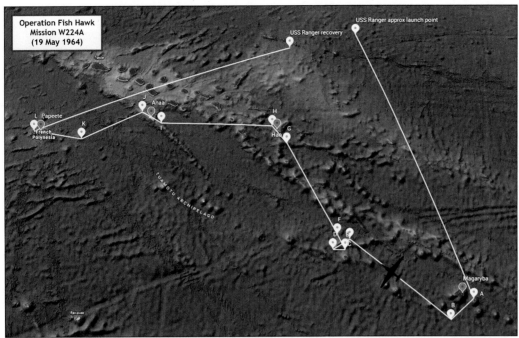

To fly over the French Polynesian test site in the remote Pacific required a carrier launch. Fish Hawk was an ideal operational test of that capability. (Map by Tom Cooper based on Data SIO, NOAA, USN, NGA, GEBCO and Landsat/Copernicus)

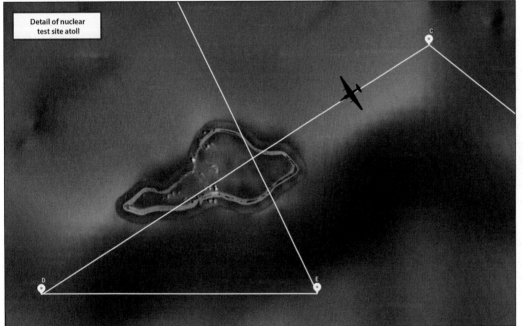

The planners expected no threat to the Fish Hawk flights as W224A overflew the atoll twice. (Map by Tom Cooper based on Data SIO, NOAA, USN, NGA, GEBCO and Landsat/Copernicus)

Operation Fish Hawk

Little more than two months later in May 1964, the US Navy and the CIA conducted the only operational use of the U-2 carrier operation concept under the unclassified code name Fish Hawk.

Det H commander Colonel William Gregory, was on board USS *Ranger* for the voyage, having selected personnel and much of the required equipment for the mission. The U-2s had quietly flown to Hickham AFB, Hawaii. Then the two U-2Gs (Art 348 and 362) flew out to join USS *Ranger*, piloted by Jim Barnes and Buster Edens. Arriving from Hawaii the two flew approaches and trapped landings onto USS *Ranger* to renew their carrier qualification.[4] Their aircraft were equipped with the newly delivered 112B/Delta II and B cameras.

The aircraft had made a radio silent arrival onto USS *Ranger* in an attempt to hide the operation. Even on the carrier, the two U-2s were kept in a 'secure area', protected by Marines. Representatives from Eastman Kodak and NPIC were on board *Ranger* to process and assess the tracker camera imagery. The main mission film was to be returned to San Diego by A-3B Skywarrior as soon as practicable. Their target was the newly constructed Polynesian nuclear test facility at Mururoa atoll in the Tuamotu archipelago. The French switched to the south Pacific after abandoning their original nuclear test site in Algeria. US intelligence agencies monitored the development of the French weapons programme. Following an announcement that Prime Minister Georges Pompidou would visit the site in July 1964, the CIA seized the opportunity to photograph the new facilities in the period before nuclear tests began.

The mission plan called for a single sortie, with the new 112B camera, and a small ELINT payload, with two backup flights in case of weather or technical issues. As USS *Ranger* approached 800 miles from the archipelago the aircraft was readied for the first flight. Two missions were planned. W224A flown by James Barnes on 19 May 1964 with Colonel Gregory recording W224A's departure at precisely 0700L . *Ranger*'s radar soon lost contact with him as Barnes climbed to 68,000ft.[5]

His task was to cover the primary objective on Mururoa, and several secondary targets, mostly other atolls including Hoa which became an advanced support base. No opposition was expected as Barnes broke the usual cardinal rule of aerial photo-reconnaissance and passed over the main target area twice. He flew over other atolls before imaging the settlement at Papeete, then turned north-eastwards to rendezvous with USS *Ranger*. He began his let down 100 miles before reaching the carrier and landed straight-on. The second mission, W234A, a repeat of the first, was flown on 22 May by Buster Edens. There had been significant cloud over some of the first mission's target areas, but by combining both days' imagery, coverage of all the primary and secondary target areas was achieved. After the completion of operations, USS *Ranger* headed to San

These two images of Mururoa have been attributed to KH-7 Mission 4037 from 26 May 1967. However, they could be 'sanitised' images from the 1964 U-2 missions but, in either case, illustrate what the Fish Hawk flights saw. The north-east corner of the atoll was likely taken as the U-2 flew its second run over the site. (NARA via Tim Brown)

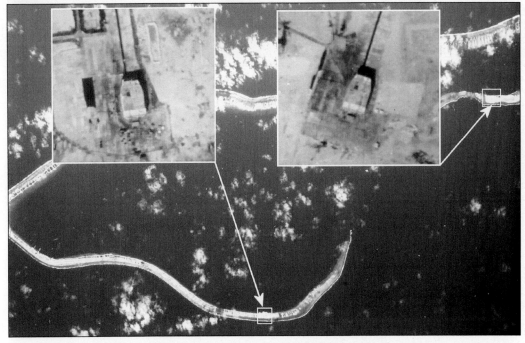

The two solid concrete blockhouses were known to the French as 'Colette' and 'Dindon' and were sometimes used for cold shot, sub-critical nuclear tests of key components. (NARA via Tim Brown)

operations (including Art 054/N810X and Art 055/N812X) with the installation of an 'RX-107' arrestor hook kit, as on the U-2G.[8] Two U-2Gs (Art 348 and 349) were placed in flyable storage in case they were required for contingency carrier operations.[9] In September, Art 055 conducted ground and flight testing at NAS Lakehurst, NJ for carrier suitability, particularly testing appropriate settings for the carriers arresting gear cables. A small 'skid' (RG297) was attached to each wingtip to help prevent cable-snagging if the wing touched the deck. This was considered an interim arrangement ahead of a lower drag design option being developed. Strengthened main gear landing struts (RL5-9) were fitted as they had better energy absorption characteristics than the original design. Another modification was the introduction of a hinged outer wing that allowed the last 70 inches to be folded inwards to ease movement in restricted spaces.[10] This was initially fitted on three aircraft, including the two adapted for carrier operations. It was later introduced across the U-2R fleet, even though rarely used.

On 20 November 1969 both U-2Rs staged to Wallops Station, VA, a NASA operated facility, for exercise 'Blue Gull V'. Prior training for the selected pilots and the assigned Navy Landing Signals Officer (LSO) saw them practise 'mirror landings' at Edwards AFB. On 21 November, Art 055 was flown by company pilot Bill Park out to USS *America* where he was responsible for qualifying the U-2R for carrier operations. Flying a couple of low approaches/wave offs he had to return to base because the tailhook would not lower. The locking pin had not been removed before his departure. Returning, he successfully trapped the cable. The handling characteristics for the U-2R for carrier operations were said to be much better than for the U-2Gs.[11] The longer wings, better flap configuration and improved throttle response all helped. After landing the pilot taxied forward after being released from the cable. He would shut down the engine as the aircraft was towed back into position for take-off. For departure the wing pogos were not fitted, instead, the right wing was held by a member of the deck crew. Park took off again using just 150–200ft of the straight deck and landed back on again. Over the next two days, Agency pilots Danny Wright

Francisco. The U-2s departed as they arrived within range of land, to touch down at NAS Almeda, then flying on to Edwards AFB.[6]

On 26 April 1965 veteran CIA pilot Buster Edens died when his U-2G crashed at Edwards AFB. He was due to carry out carrier landing practice on the simulated deck constructed there. On his first approach, he was told to cut power and extend spoilers by the LSO. On touchdown, his left wing touched the runway and dragged along it for some 50ft. Edens applied power and got airborne again and was told to gain altitude and check his aircraft. Just two miles from the control tower he appeared to enter a low-level spin and hit the ground.[7]

USS America

When the remaining 'small wing' U-2s were being replaced by the new U-2R, three of the new aircraft were modified for carrier

Wing folding mechanism revealed on NASA's U-2/ER-2 N706NA (Art 063) in 2005. When the upper wing bolts were released, the wing was extended a few inches and swung slightly forward a few inches on hinges and could then be folded. Before all of that the trailing edge of the outer panel had to be secured in place to stop it from flapping around. (Brian Lockett)

Art 055/N812X approaches touchdown on USS *America*, the only known time the U-2R went to sea with the CIA. (NARA)

and Ben Higgins, plus RAF pilots Squadron Leaders Harry Drew and Dick Cloke, each successfully made four landings to complete their carrier qualification. On the final day, Park completed the 'heavy' take-off test requirement with 2,088 gallons of fuel, with the detachable pogos fitted. Care was taken to ensure the fuel load was evenly balanced in the aircraft's wing tanks to ensure a wings-level departure and avoid any adverse effects if the deck pitched during take-off. Full power applied and 100ft into the run the right pogo dropped off and the left at 200ft as the aircraft climbed steeply away and headed towards the shore.

The tests were undoubtedly successful although minor damage was sustained. One of the wingtip deflectors, fitted to avoid cable-snagging if a wing touched the deck was slightly damaged on Park's initial landing.[12] Arrestor cable-whip caused minor damage to the rear undercarriage doors and one of the door struts, even though it was protected by a deflector. There were minor dents on the fuselage underside caused by the hook bouncing off the deck during landings.

Below deck stowage of the larger U-2R had to be even more precise than on the U-2G. The aircraft was positioned precisely opposite the aircraft carrier's side lift, using deck marked lines. The outer wing

Art 055 on USS *America*'s flight deck. The picture was probably taken after the initial deck landing by company pilot Bill Park. Visible is the wing tip cable deflector. (NARA)

Prepared for its final take-off from USS *America*, fully loaded with fuel for the flight home meant both pogos were fitted. For other missions, just one was used. (NARA)

panels were folded. The two undercarriage legs were then rotated through 90 degrees and the aircraft manually pushed sideways onto the lift. The clearance was just two feet at the front and one foot at the rear. To clear the deck edge when the lift was lowered, the main wheels had to be pushed to within 4ft 6in of the lift's outer edge. To ensure it did not tip over into the sea 250lb of ballast weighted the inboard wingtip. That also caused the fuel to flow into the left wing weighing it down still further. Below deck it was pushed off the lift into position, the whole process taking 55 minutes. When returning the aircraft to the deck it was secured onto the lift and wing stands

placed under each wing to ensure the inboard wing did not touch the deck this time.[13]

Although the trials worked, US Navy enthusiasm was waning suggesting that the cost of U-2 operations would likely not be worth the effort. When the deck was rigged for U-2 operations routine flying for other fixed-wing types was all but impossible. More importantly, when a US Carrier Group is on the move, there is a whole armada of warships, supply vessels and submarines that travel with it to protect and keep it ready for operations. To take a carrier to a location where a U-2 could fly aboard, steam to an operating area

U-2R on the flight deck of USS *America* ready for departure. (NARA)

and conduct just one, or at most a few flights, was a huge resource cost. As satellite imagery vastly improved during the 1960s the prospects for using a U-2 from an aircraft carrier dwindled and the costs became increasingly prohibitive. However, Det G maintained its carrier deployment kit beyond 1971.[14]

6
NEW AND IMPROVED: THE U-2R

The original combined USAF and Agency purchase of 55 U-2As had been continually eroded by significant losses over the years and by the end of 1966 was down to just 17 airframes. Four CIA aircraft were with Det G at Edwards, two in Taiwan and three more under repair. The remainder belonged to SAC. Aircraft had been loaned between the two over the years for various projects – Agency airframes were better equipped than USAF ones. However, it was clear the fleet was approaching critical numbers and new airframes were necessary if the U-2 was to remain viable as a type.

New Model
The U-2R was a major redesign of the original airframe. Its wings were 23 feet longer at 103ft, with 40 percent greater surface area than the U-2C. A more powerful and improved performance engine compared to the original J-57, plus two pressurised equipment bays and a better cockpit layout. It was still a difficult machine to handle and required advanced flying skills and experience to fly effectively. Its Pratt & Whitney J75-P-13B engine and greatly increased fuel capacity enabled the U-2R to climb well above the admitted 74,000ft ceiling in the right conditions and had an endurance over seven hours and mission ranges of around 3,000nm. It had larger control surfaces and a greater airspeed window between stall and buffet onset, which made flying it a little easier.

The fuel system was redesigned to smooth the aircraft's centre of gravity shifts, as fuel burned off. It effectively allowed fuel to drain from the outer wing tanks to the inner wing and into the main fuel

and sump tanks, mounted in the fuselage. During flights, fuel from the inner wing tanks was used first. Fuel in the smaller capacity outer wing tanks was held there. This helped keep the wing more rigid and reduced wing bending until the pilot was ready to open the drain valves once the main tank fuel levels got much lower. The main fuel tank was in the fuselage, with a 99-gallon sump tank, the fuel reserve.

The U-2R's fuselage was wider and around 25 percent longer than the earlier models. The mission equipment load increased to a maximum of just over 1,000lb that could be split between the pressurised equipment Q-bay and the new, distinctively shaped and interchangeable nose. Initially, antennae were mostly flush-mounted and wherever possible blended into the fuselage and wing leading edge. System XX, a rearward looking fighter engine IR plume sensor, was built into the wing trailing edge. System XXI was a compact COMINT receiver. Existing systems, like Birdwatcher, were further enhanced.

The larger cockpit allowed an improved instrument layout and gave more space. This allowed pilots to wear the bulkier but more comfortable David Clark Company S1010 full pressure suit and a full zero-zero ejector seat was fitted. The drift sight remained invaluable and the astronavigation sextant finally dispensed with. New Doppler, TACAN and beacon-based navigation equipment were installed and the aircraft's radios improved.

Work had begun on the new version in late 1965, with the first U-2R (Art 051/68-10329) flying on 28 August 1967. Following

'New and Improved', the U-2R prototype (Art 051/N803X) takes off from the desert on 28 August 1968. Later reworked to full production standard, it had a distinguished operational career. (Lockheed)

The U-2R (right) is considerably larger than its forerunner the U-2C (left) with 23ft longer wings giving them a 40 percent greater area. (USAF Museum)

the flight test programme's commencement, further airframe modifications were made to resolve a tendency to veer on take-off and reduce the engine noise. The test programme was completed in 1968 and the last of a combined Agency order for five U-2Rs and seven for the USAF was delivered on 11 December 1968.[1] The USAF had not initially been interested in the U-2R, joining the programme later, in much the same way as they had done with the U-2A back in 1956. Later the USAF purchased an additional 37 U-2Rs built between 1981 and 1989.

The modifications built into the U-2R reflected changes to the main tasks it was now being called upon to perform. Whilst overflight missions could still be flown, they were most likely only to be undertaken in permissive environments, where there was no significant threat of being shot down. The U-2R was to act more as a stand-off, often littoral, platform for both photographic and electronic reconnaissance. Its unique contribution to the 'game' was

that it operated at very high altitude, so was able to see and listen over much greater distances than more comprehensively equipped platforms like the many variants of the RC-135. In just a few years it became even more flexible, able to collect intelligence and transmit data across the world, via satellites or linked ground stations in near real time. However, these capabilities would only be valuable if the U-2R's sensors continued to be capable of collecting relevant intelligence.

U-2s Compared

Retired USAF U-2R pilots Lieutenant Colonel Bruce Jinneman and Lieutenant Colonel Rick Bishop spoke to the author bout some of the major differences between the U-2C and U-2R, both having flown the C model during their training, before flying the TR-1/U-2R operationally for much of their careers.

After his interview flights and acceptance to SAC's U-2 programme, Rick Bishop commenced training in February 1979. As well as flying the two-seat U-2CT, early training flights included flying one of the few still airworthy U-2Cs. His headline comparison was that:

The U-2C was a Porsche 930-T. The U-2R was an 8-Series-M, BMW. And, each Dragon Lady had her unique personality. My flight log states: "First flight in the C... What a Performer!" The max gross weight of the U-2C was about 24,000lbs. versus 40,000lb for the U-2R utilizing the same engine. It could easily outclimb and fly about 3,000ft higher than the R. I flew C Model 56-6701 [Art 368] on high flights and 56-6953 and 56-6692 [Art 393 and Art 359 the U-2Cs converted to U-2CTs] and again later when I was an Instructor Pilot and lead for VIP and Interview Acceptance Flights. There were only eight of the original 12 R models and two each of Cs and CTs left when I arrived at Beale. That was the entire U-2 fleet except for a couple of Cs with NASA.

The C was a lot lighter on the controls than the R. That being said, landing the C was a nightmare compared to the R with its roll and landing spoilers. '953, in particular, had an early baffling system that allowed wing fuel to flow outboard when one wing was low and inboard on the high wing if it was not kept precisely wings-level after landing. Once the wing skid made contact with the runway, one of two options had to be executed immediately; either application of full power, in hopes of gaining enough airspeed for the aileron to lift the heavy wing or abort the touch and go landing. More than a few ended up either in the weeds, off the edge of the runway, or became airborne at a wild angle from the runway heading!

At altitude, the C was more responsive, but could get into a Dutch-Roll situation very easily, which required counteracting rudder inputs to correct it. Since it had only an 80-foot wingspan, critical Mach and stall speed got dangerously close in the "coffin corner," also known as "the throat," when they were separated by only +/- 2–3 knots. Hand flying was very tedious and best left to the autopilot if it was operational.

Bruce Jinneman's experiences were in a similar vein. He explained:

The U-2C was a "squirrelly" airplane because, with its shorter wingspan, about 40% smaller than the R and was rather overpowered. When you flew the C model lightweight, there were throttle gates, that rather sensibly limited us to about 90% power. If we went beyond those to full power, it gave a better than 1:1 thrust ratio and you could really stand the airplane on its tail and go straight up. It had a much crisper response to its flight controls, just because of its shorter wing. It could also be a very dangerous aircraft to fly in the traffic pattern. If you were not careful, it could get away from you. That being said it was like driving a sports car, compared to the R model. If you were comfortable with it, the C was just a joy to fly.

Bruce explained one of the U-2C's more unusual features.

The seats in the C were not adjustable. There was maximum height for pilots, something I guess around six feet, but I was 5ft 8in. So what they did for us shorter people was to put pieces of plywood under the seat to lift us higher. Talking with Rick he was a four-plywood pilot and I was something like six-sheets. The R model was the first to have an adjustable up and down seat.

Rick Bishop continued: 'For our 'High missions' (above 70,000ft) training we flew Photo Flight Line (PFL, pronounced 'Piffle') navigation in the C model. The C required the unpleasant use of the old partial pressure suit which was skin-tight when deflated and contracted even more when pressurisation was lost.'

Bruce described the discomfort in more detail:

The early design partial pressure suits were very uncomfortable. It was like being squeezed into a girdle over your whole body. Once you got it on, they even tightened it some more. When you got back from a high flight and removed the suit you had welts up and down your arms and on your legs. It looked as if someone had beaten you with a stick. It was horrible. I had 8-10 flights in the C model, then my first flight in the R.

He contrasted that with the U-2R's cockpit where:

We wore a full pressure suit because of the extreme altitudes we operated at. It was a pain to get on. We had to have a couple of people help us, but once fitted in the suit it was pretty comfortable. We pre-breathed 100 percent oxygen for the hour before take-off. Once ready it was out to the aeroplane to strap in. Inside the cockpit, movement was limited but we could just about comfortably reach all the aircraft instruments. It was like flying airline economy class on a long non-stop journey, without the luxury of being able to get up and walk around.

Given how tough the U-2 was to fly manually for long periods, a well-functioning autopilot was vital. Bruce explained that:

The autopilot was never one of the strong suits of the U-2. When you engaged it you had controls for pitch and yaw. You could set those quite firmly so the airplane did not drift much. But when you then hit some turbulence or air temperature changes, the autopilot kept constantly adjusting, trying to keep to the settings you had input. Then you would get a very bumpy ride until it gave up and just kicked out the autopilot. So you always had to pay attention and adjust the potentiometers to get the best ride.

Asked about the noise levels in the U-2's cockpit, Bruce explained: 'The only sound that could be heard was the oxygen entering, then exhaled, from the helmet. Even the engine, creating near maximum power, was just a whisper in the background.'

Both men reported that the U-2C could be a challenge to land. Rick described how it was explained for his first flight:

[It was] an absolute necessity to stall the aircraft at exactly three feet above the runway. If the stall did not occur before contact with the runway, the U-2 'skipped' back into the air, just three feet or less. That required a stalled condition to be re-established before touchdown. A 'bounce' occurred when the plane exceeded four-feet. That required an aggressive push forward on the control yoke to prevent a stall, followed immediately by full back pressure to initiate the stall again at three feet. This action occurred in a split second and was usually initiated by the IP in the front seat of the U-2CT. Any stall above four feet usually resulted in structural damage to the landing gear or airframe.

Bruce continued:

The C model carried a drag chute for short field landings. You released the chute about two feet above the ground. It stalled the aircraft and you landed. The other situation in which you used it, was for no flap landings at standard airfields. You would pop the chute after touchdown and once the speed dropped to 30–40kts you released it and let it drift away. It was much trickier landing the C than the R model.

Evolving Payloads

In the mid-1960s, several new sensors were nearly ready to enter service with the U-2Cs. Several of them were soon adapted for use by the U-2R. Until 1965, the mainstay of the U-2's photographic capability was the B camera. After its early problems, reliability was significantly improved and provided high-quality imagery. The early Long Range Oblique Photography (LOROP) C camera had been abandoned in 1959. As James Baker had discovered in the 1950s constructing his massive 240in focal length lens, vibrations made much of the imagery unusable. Despite investing considerable effort and using a 21-man team from March to December 1958 the problem of 'vibration induced image degradation' was never satisfactorily solved.[2] Along with its abandonment went most of the hopes of ever being able to perform very long-distance stand-off photography. That would become a more pressing issue again into the 1960s, as overflight missions became much riskier to mount with successful employment of the SA-2 by the Chinese and Russians.

System 112 (ITEK 'Delta') Series

The next generation camera was known as 'System 112A' or 'ITEK Delta 1'. The simplest description is as an adaption of the camera carried by the KH-3/4 Corona reconnaissance satellites that had entered service in August 1960. A 1959 engineering design study explored the many issues involved and considerable effort was expended trying to determine what useful data the Soviets might be able to gather about the Corona satellites' capabilities if a System 112 camera was brought down in a U-2 over their territory.[3] The camera used a 24-inch f3.5 'Petzval' design lens to obtain stereo photography. It comprised two lenses, one forward, tilted 13 degrees frontwards and the other 13 degrees backwards that gave overlapping coverage across a 70-degree arc beneath the aircraft and provided the stereographic effect. From about 70,000ft it covered a 16.5nm-wide strip by one mile deep. It could be adjusted to give different amounts of imagery overlap. An inherent feature of the Petzval type lens design is that its sharpest focus is at the very centre, becoming softer towards the edge. It carried up to 7,800ft of 70mm film.

System 112A was tested in September 1963 and first used operationally over Cuba in October for USAF Brass Knob missions. Unfortunately, it had to be removed from the aircraft after just the third mission (3761) and returned to ITEK for rework following an inverter failure that had overloaded the camera's electrical systems. The first operational use in the Far East was for Mission 6070 on 29 December 1963 (and again the following day) when pilots Al Rand and James Bedford launched from Takhli flying over Vietnam, Laos and Cambodia. Its use by Dets G and H in the Far East was quite limited, where the priority tended to be area coverage rather than great detail of directly overflown targets.[4]

This was followed by System 112B (ITEK 'Delta II'). The CIA purchased four of these cameras delivered in March, April, May and June 1964. In common with most of the U-2's cameras, they required a unique design hatch cover. This version could continuously cover 2,634 miles of territory 17 miles wide if required. At its best, the camera achieved a one-foot resolution directly underneath the

aircraft and was often carried in conjunction with System VI.[5] Two Delta II versions were further modified by ITEK and held by Det H. The 'Delta III' was the ultimate development of this camera. It covered a 16nm swathe of ground from 70,000ft, used 7,800ft film and weighed 432lb.[6]

FD-4 IR Scanner

An infrared camera system was developed by Texas Instruments, primarily intended to image subjects with high 'thermal energy' such as nuclear reactors. Two were purchased for U-2 use. It weighed 120lb and had a 100-degree field of view that produced imagery covering a 28-mile band at 70,000ft. It could be carried in addition to a B camera. The system was not particularly successful, with a 35ft space between objects necessary to achieve adequate resolution. As mentioned previously, it was used for two aborted missions aimed at the Soviet-built Lanzhou uranium enrichment facility in November 1964. Another sortie in January 1965 was more successful, but Mission C025C on 10 January 1965, was lost and pilot Jack Chang captured by the Chinese when he targeted the Baotou plutonium manufacturing facility.

Little is known about additional infrared cameras used by the U-2, the FFD-2, FFD-3 and FFD-4. In 1965 new hatches were authorised for the FFD-4 camera on the U-2. Understood to be a stereo device, the sensor and associated recorder weighed 160lb, replaced the tracker camera and incorporated antenna for System VI and the Oscar Sierra too.[7] The device was later adapted for use for the Lockheed A-12/SR-71 'Oxcart'.

Lightweight B Camera

An improved 'B2' model began replacing the traditional B camera in 1966. At approximately 455lb it weighed 90lb less than the original and brought across the board improvements including better ground resolution, increased by around 25 percent and even greater reliability.[8]

The B2 used an f10, 36-inch lens. From 70,000ft, in Mode 1, the lateral coverage was a remarkable 563nm, of which it was said, 154 miles worth across could be usefully interpreted. It could do that continuously for five hours 42 minutes or 2,230nm. Mode 2 took a much narrower swathe of 19 miles across for nine hours 36 minutes or 3,755nm of much higher quality. Film capacity was still two 6,500ft-long rolls of 9.5-inch film and an achievable resolution of 12 to 18 inches.[9] Soon after the introduction of the B2, the next generation of U-2 camera, the 'Optical Bar Camera' was under development.

H Camera

Efforts to develop a new generation of U-2 long range oblique photographic equipment peaked with Hycon's 'H' camera. It consisted of a 66-inch, f5 auto-focus folded optic lens and carried 2,000ft of five-inch square film. It weighed around 666lb fully loaded and was stabilised by three gyros, aimed from the cockpit using the Mk IV hand control, using the U-2's drift sight. It covered up to 70 degrees each side of the aircraft, a swathe of imagery 31.6nm wide from 70,000ft.[10] The weight and size of the system meant only it and a tracker camera could be carried, precluding installation of major SIGINT payloads.

Just three H cameras were built, one allocated to Det H, a spare and the other to SAC. It operated well only within very tight parameters. The power of the camera meant it had to be very carefully aimed to successfully capture specific targets. Aircraft handling had to be precise to not exceed the H's yaw and roll stops. The camera structure and lens needed to be kept within a 2.5 degrees Celsius temperature range for two hours before photography otherwise sharp focus was lost. The three gyros that stabilised the camera periodically failed and were difficult and expensive to replace at $4,498 each.[11] SAC soon gave up their H camera as they found it difficult to successfully operate and it was placed in reserve with Det G at Edwards AFB.

A November 1969 report indicates the H camera's performance was initially disappointing because the Det H U-2Rs were now required to perform peripheral missions 20 miles offshore:

> The present standoff mode has resulted in long oblique photos of a relatively narrow band along [the Chinese coast] and has increased the problems of ground haze and terrain masking. These problems were further compounded by changing from the 3-8 foot average resolution of the HR73B ('B' configuration) camera system to the 6-8 foot estimated resolution of the 111B ('H' configuration) camera system. Stated in terms of interpretability, this means from good to poor resolution or from specific identification of essential elements of information to 'probable vehicles and/or equipment'.[12]

Even given such constraints, the H camera was considered irreplaceable. As an Agency paper explained: 'Maintaining the 'H' camera in the OSA inventory is not justified on the basis of its annual cost or the number of operational missions it has been used on, but rather from the fact that we do not have any camera that will do a peripheral or stand-off mission as well'.[13] It was certainly essential to Det H's operations off the PRC and Vietnamese coasts, used on over 70 known peripheral missions between 1968 and the detachment's closure in 1974. Much later, during Operation Desert Storm in 1991, the H camera was used for over 25 missions producing impressive overhead photography but much lower value oblique imagery.

ITEK's IRIS II Camera

The ITEK produced IRIS II (KA-80A) became available from late 1968, with 13 purchased (six CIA, six USAF and one spare) it has remained in service for occasional use for nearly 50 years. Also referred to as an Optical Bar Camera (OBC), it was a major step forward in design as used on the 'Key-Hole' photographic satellites like the KH-8 Gambit and KH-9 Hexagon. The traditional shutter based camera takes an image and then, moving the film across a glass platen, takes another image and repeats the process. This method often experiences problems of shutter vibration that affects the sharpness of the images. Oversimplified, the OBC has a 'Petzval' design lens. Instead of having a conventional shutter it uses a slit opening that admits light to expose the film.[14] In this design, the lens continuously rotates, but only collects images as it passes the open 'slit'. That eliminated much of the traditional vibration and with precisely calculated 'image movement compensation' to allow for the forward movement of the camera, greatly improved the quality of the imagery produced. Rather than providing a mosaic of traditional single pictures, it provided long strips of images that could be greatly enlarged. Transforming what sounds like a simple idea into an operational system was in reality extremely complex. It was a more automated system than most of the earlier cameras and required very precise design, construction and synchronisation of all the equipment's components.

The IRIS II OBC for the U-2 was originally fitted with a 24-inch f3.5 lens and described as a 'lightweight panoramic camera' that weighed around 395lb. Up to 10,500ft of five-inch-wide film could produce about 2,300nm of stereographic imagery, or 3,700nm

The Optical Bar Camera (OBC), introduced in 1968, was winched into a U-2S in March 2011 at Osan AB in the same way as the original A camera payload in 1956. (USAF Sgt Paul Holcomb)

of standard imagery. Because of the camera's complex design, it embodied a lot more electronic circuitry than its predecessors. It required more specialised management and ground handling equipment at its operating bases, than the traditional cameras used by the U-2. The OBC was also used by the SR-71.

As the U-2's overflight operations declined the need for the highest specification of camera declined too. The OBC takes images across a 50nm swathe at 70,000ft with a very respectable 9-inch resolution in the vertical.[15] It has remained useful and in recent years has continued to be used for unclassified activities such as disaster relief support missions, including monitoring typhoon and earthquake damage.

New Electronic Equipment

Unfortunately, details of the original U-2R's electronic sensors and self-defence equipment remain sparse. HRB-Singer's System XVII was a wideband SIGINT sensor system covering VHF to X-band signals, with direction-finding ability. First designed in the early

Once the OBC camera is installed, the U-2's external hatch cover is manoeuvred into position. (USAF Sergeant Paul Holcomb)

U-2R Arrives in Taiwan

Rotating Agency aircraft between the US and Taoyuan was a major task in its own right and generally used the operation name 'Swap Shop'. This was well illustrated with the transition from the U-2C and U-2R in Taiwan. As well as bringing the aircraft, there was the necessity to move extra equipment required for the new variant too. Originally planned for late 1968 the programme finally slipped into 1969. 'Swap Shop 11' called for the U-2Rs to fly from California to Hickam AFB, on Hawaii, then to Andersen AFB, Guam and finally on to Taiwan. At each stopover location, the CIA wanted to minimalise their presence. The KC-135As usually carried the necessary equipment for these movements, but the specialist items now required for the new U-2R meant extra airlift capacity was necessary. Everything also had to be moved in such a way that if one of the U-2s developed a fault en route to Taiwan, adequate spares and support equipment was available on a support KC-135A to minimise the time it would spend on the ground at an unusual airfield. By 1968 a portable 'Birdwatcher' station had been manufactured and could be installed in a KC-135A. This allowed better monitoring of the U-2's critical systems on the long Pacific transit. The two U-2R replacements arrived in Taiwan during January (Art 057) and February 1969 (Art 058). The remaining U-2C (Art 383) was returned to the US in a C-124 during the first quarter of 1969.[17]

1960s, it was continuously improved. In the U-2R the equipment was nose-mounted with the antenna in the wings. The self-defence System XX was fitted to CIA U-2Rs from 1968. Its main sensor component was fitted on the trailing edge of the wing and looked behind the aircraft, designed to acquire and counter the guidance radars carried by MiG fighters. System XXI was a TRW developed compact COMINT receiver to capture air defence voice communications, not often a high priority for Agency operations. System XXII has been described simply as a 'jammer' to defeat air-to-air missiles. The quality of electronic sensors systems caught up with the U-2R's ability to carry them in the 1980s, as digital electronics matured. They were used with the Air Force TR-1s, deployed to the UK in the 1980s with its Senior Spear, ASARS-2 and SYERS payloads.[16]

Peripheral Programme

The premier operational U-2R mission from Taiwan is recorded as C069C on 8 April 1969 and was pilot Tao 'Tom' Wang's first operational flight. His four hours 35 minutes mission in Art 058

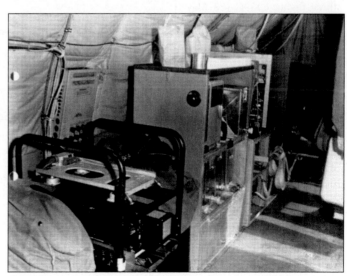

The deployment of the first U-2Rs to Taiwan in early 1969 saw a KC-135A carrying extra equipment required for the R model and a portable Birdwatcher system to monitor critical data from the U-2R as it progressed across the Pacific. (CIA)

took him along the PRC coast, south of Taiwan, equipped with the 'H' camera.[18] Over the next five years up to May 1974, the U-2Rs and Taiwanese pilots flew approximately 122 such peripheral missions covering the whole coast of mainland China. These were a mixture of SIGINT and photographic missions. Most carried the new H camera; others used a specialist SIGINT fit called 'Long Shaft'.

Early 1971 saw another aircraft exchange with 'Swap Shop 12'. Art 053 was delivered to Taiwan in January 1971 and Art 058 headed in the opposite direction, returning to Lockheed at Palmdale, presumably for deep maintenance and further modification. Swap Shop 13 flew Art 051 to Taiwan in March 1971. This was a replacement for Art 057 in which Major Chi Hsien 'Denny' Wang had died in a landing accident at Taoyuan on 24 November 1970.[19]

Mission Routes

The U-2Rs mainly employed variations of three principal routes for their PRC coastal missions: northern, central and southern. Detailed route coordinates for most missions remain secret, but a few examples have escaped into the public domain. Routes for three flights C119C (28 May 1969), C169C (17 August 1969) and C050C (26 March 1970) are representative of the three regular routes and are shown for comparative purposes.

Mission C119C was a central coastal flight. After departing Taoyuan pilot Chungli 'Johnny' Shen flew north over the East China Sea, out of PRC radar coverage, turned into the coast at a

Representative comparison of northern, central and southern coastal routes along the PRC flown by Det H pilots in 1969–1970. (Map by Tom Cooper)

selected point and followed the coast southwards. He flew close to Shanghai and across the over 50-mile-wide entrance to Hangzhou Bay. This route immediately illustrates some of the dilemmas faced by mission planners and pilots. The U-2Rs were required to keep 20 miles from the mainland. There was some consideration, within the 303 Committee, to add an extra 12 miles distance from offshore islands. To have done this for C119C would have kept Shen over 66nm from the centre of Shanghai. In not applying the coastal islands distance provision, the pilot was no more than 40 miles from central Shanghai. In some instances, the additional 12 miles beyond the coastal islands would have put the U-2s over 60 miles from the mainland coast. Powerful as the H camera was, the CIA's estimates indicated that this would have degraded target coverage between 37 to 52 percent, because of these increased stand-off distances. To this could be added a further unpredictable amount of image degradation due to increased oblique angle of the photography (particularly significant if hills or mountainous terrain was involved) and the greater effects of coastal atmospheric haze. That would likely have made considerable amounts of imagery largely worthless.[20] Shen's flight was roughly 650 miles from north to south before he broke off, close to Dongshandao, and headed back to Taoyuan. The 'entry' and 'exit' points for these coastal missions were no doubt different for each flight.

Central and southern routes could overlap considerably. For example, C169C on 17 August 1969. After departing Taoyuan, the pilot of Art 058, with an H camera and System XVIIB payload, flew down to the north-east of Hainan Island before approaching the coast following it round before he directly overflew central Hong Kong, still then under British control. From there he could see further inland towards PRC military installations bordering the colony and the city of Guangzhou. It is not known to what extent the British were informed about the overflight or may have seen any of the resulting imagery. Returning over water he followed the coastline past the heavily defended coastal mainland zone. Roughly abeam Foochow (Fuzhou) he broke off and recovered to Taoyuan, a 1,530-mile flight that lasted four hours 25 minutes. Other missions on this southern route specifically targeted Hainan Island and beyond.

The northern route for Mission C050C, on 26 March 1970, is intriguing too. It essentially followed an irregular circuit over part of the Yellow Sea paralleling the coastline, passing Dalian (Port Arthur) and placed the U-2R between coastal islands and the mainland on two occasions. The lack of previous waypoints for the flight from A to H, plus the fact that its first plot point is roughly abeam the North Korean and South Korean border, is perhaps indicative that the mission staged from, or into, South Korea, rather than Taoyuan,

considerably reducing an otherwise 2,000-mile round trip, or at least wanted to give that impression. We know from Mike Hua that occasionally the Taiwanese conducted staging operations from Kunsan AB as early as March 1963.[21] Osan AB in South Korea became a USAF U-2 operating base from 1976.

Whilst peripheral flights were not in such great danger of being shot down these missions still faced fighter and SAM threats and were not without incident. There were persistent concerns that SAM missiles could be placed on some of the offshore coastal islands to bring down another U-2. The best-documented example that it has been possible to piece together comes from 1 December 1969 and Mission C299C. Tom Wang departed Taoyuan at 0200Z headed along the coast of Zhejiang province and turned his H camera on at 0313Z.

Data collected from his tracker camera suggested that he took a 'shortcut' making his route more direct and went from Point G towards Point I, missing out H. Doing so probably made his intentions clearer to the PRC forces watching his progress on their air defence radars. That slight change of plan was nearly fatal. Three SA-2s fired at Wang's aircraft causing him to make a drastic evasive manoeuvre, and a missile exploded off his right wing. That sudden change in course and altitude is reflected in the images recorded by the tracker camera. It captured his position every 30 seconds and from that analysts accurately calculated his actual position. The tracker even recorded one of the missiles in flight.[22] To his great credit, Wang continued the mission! According to a CIA Deputy Director's report a few months later: 'A previously undetected, hastily-prepared [SA-2] site on Ssu Chiao (sic) Island' was discovered. A precise location is even suggested for the SA-2 site although, if accurate, nothing of it is now visible on modern satellite imagery. If it was only a temporary site we should not expect to see anything so many years later. However, two close-by hilltop sites

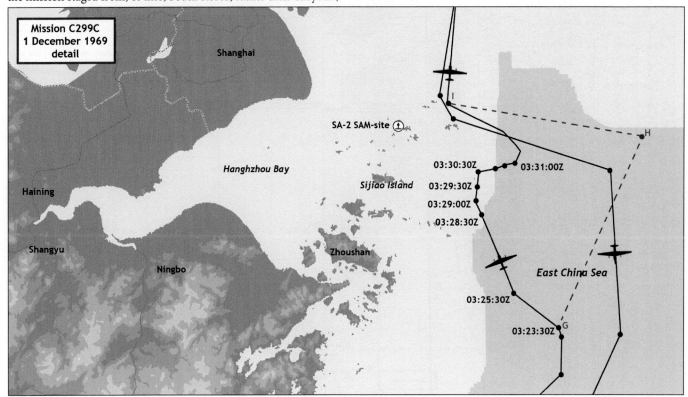

Pilot Tom Wang took a nearly fatal 'shortcut' in his planned route for mission C299C, missing out point H, instead attempting to head directly from point G to I. Determined later from the aircraft's tracker camera, his actual route took him much closer to the coastal islands as he headed towards point I. The numbers indicate the time images were taken by the tracking camera. (Map by Tom Cooper based on Landsat/Copernicus, Data SIO, USN, NGA, GEBCO)

Mission C042C

This U-2R flight was targeted against communist Chinese airfields along the central coastal belt of the PRC close to Taiwan. It took off from Taoyuan airfield on 16 January 1972, carrying an H camera for photography.

NPIC Mission Coverage Plots were produced for consumption by parts of the intelligence community. The photographic coverage was plotted onto the appropriate USAF World Aeronautical Charts. Here is a composite of the three maps covered by the flightpath of C042C flying a course parallel but no closer than, 20 miles to the Chinese coast. By now the imagery taken was far more selectively. The areas photographed are shown shaded. C042C photographed 29 of the 77 COMIREX targets and found 13 bonus ones 'between Shanghai south and the Quemoy Islands.'

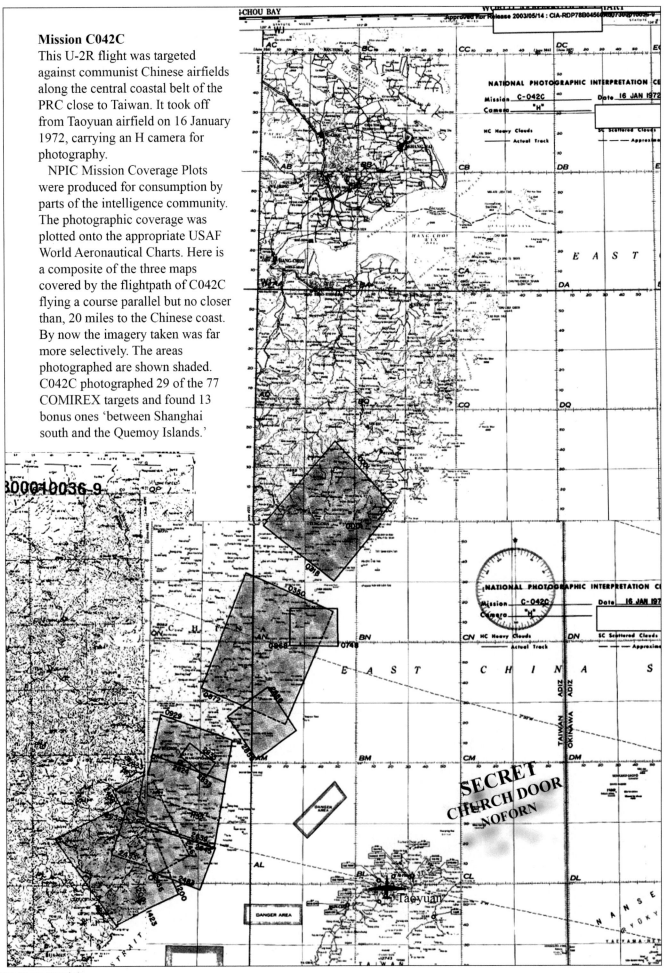

(CIA/Kevin Wright)

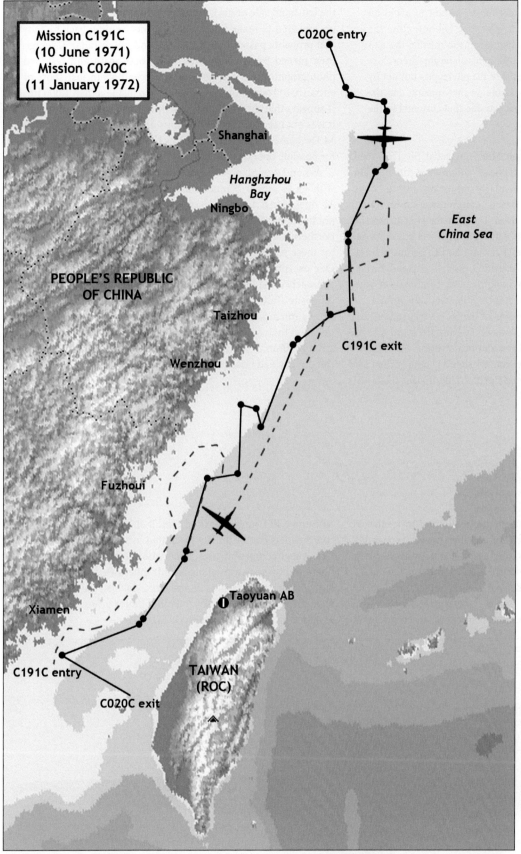

Mission C191C (10 June 1971)
Mission C020C (11 January 1972)

C020C entry

Shanghai

Hanghzhou Bay

Ningbo

East China Sea

PEOPLE'S REPUBLIC OF CHINA

Taizhou

C191C exit

Wenzhou

Fuzhoui

Xiamen

Taoyuan AB

C191C entry

TAIWAN (ROC)

C020C exit

When the Long Shaft SIGINT system was carried the H camera had to be left behind. However, for two missions (C141C and C191C) in mid-1971 it was used together with a modified B camera that produced poor results. This is compared with the route for Mission C020C which was a more typical Long Shaft only mission and meant the U-2R could remain further away from the PRC's coast. (Map by Tom Cooper based on Landsat/Copernicus, Data SIO, USN, NGA and GEBCO)

Chinese MiGs posed potential problems for the U-2s, although they were relatively safe at their operational altitudes, as long as they did not have a flameout. The Chinese fighters rarely zoom climbed to the U-2's altitude in an attempt to ram them, cause jet exhaust turbulence, or get a lock on with their air-to-air missiles. However, U-2 mission planning started to require the identification of potential fighter bases (as well as the SAM sites) along proposed routes. This was intended to further reduce risk wherever possible.

Mission C111C on 29 April 1971, was a northern route peripheral photographic and SIGINT flight into the Yellow Sea that took the aircraft within range of MiG-21 bases at Tsang Hsien and Ku Cheng. At some stage, either as Johnny Shen entered or left the areas near Tsingtao (most likely on the return leg), his System XX detected a heat source on his left side. He turned to point the U-2's exhaust away from the pursuing fighter. The warning light went out, but after he resumed his original course the warning came on again, to the right this time. The pilot made a right turn and heard a loud noise, seeing a silver MiG-21 zoom up less than 500ft from his right wing, at their 73,000ft altitude, and then dropping away.[23] Nevertheless, he covered 29 of the programmed targets and another 35 'bonus' targets including a new SA-2 site and two submarines at Hsiao-Ping-Tao naval base. His mission ended with a further minor drama when his U-2's brakes failed during his landing roll because of a fractured brake line. He stop-cocked the engine and came to a safe halt, merely suffering the indignity of having to be towed off the runway.

Photographic Interpreter Colonel Roy Stanley recorded an instance when processing the imagery from a CHURCH DOOR mission. This may even have been Mission C111C. They noticed how the U-2 pilot:

have signs of military occupation, one now houses what appears to be a dome covered radar.

Had snapped his plane …off track for an instant to avoid an enemy fighter in a zoom-climb. We couldn't tell how close the fighter had come, but certainly, like a ballistic missile, the Chi Com pilot would have had no control of his plane anywhere close to 70,000ft. In any case, he had missed the intercept – but not by much…There were no other incidents on that mission and the aircraft flew straight and level. That was one cool customer in the cockpit.[24]

In Spring 1971 the 600lb Long Shaft specialist SIGINT load arrived, believed to be a 'radio-telephone' microwave interception system. This would have been particularly important with the huge expansion of PRC microwave-based communication systems, especially in air defence related uses. The first mission using the system was on 7 May 1971 (C121C) along the central coastal area. When Long Shaft was carried the H camera had to be left behind, or vice versa, as together they exceeded overall payload limits. However, it was possible to carry Long Shaft in combination with one of the lighter B2 cameras. This combination was sub-optimal, as the B2 camera did not have the 'reach' of the H. It was used on just two missions in mid-1971. C141C was on 26 May 1971 and C191C on 10 June 1971, repeated almost the identical routes.[25] C141C was also pilot Chu Chien's first operational mission. He approached the PRC coast near Xiamen and headed north taking images from just

the left-hand side of his U-2. After passing out of the Taiwan Straits, he appeared to make a feint, as if he was heading back to Taoyuan and probably passed out of PRC ground-based radar coverage. He then turned back towards the PRC coast again and resumed his photographic coverage before breaking off again just short of the entrance to Hangzhou Bay having taken just less than 1,000 images. It appears that the combination may not have been worthwhile and it was not used for further missions until an apparent single-use on 14 December 1973 when the unit's H camera was forward deployed for possible operations following the Yom Kippur War.[26]

When Long Shaft was first introduced it experienced problems with its electrical components.[27] Details indicate that there were 32 operational Long Shaft missions. In a similar fashion to the photographic flights, Long Shaft SIGINT missions appear to have northern, central and southern routes too. However, details available for these routes are almost totally absent from the public domain. One exception is Mission C020C from 11 January 1972. Its route approached the PRC coast near Shanghai in the north to Quanzhou (opposite Taiwan) where it breaks off its surveillance, its route closely mirrors those for the photographic missions. It approaches no closer than approximately 30nm at its nearest point, but averages around 50nm, roughly 15nm further out to sea than the usual H camera payload missions.

7
HEADING TOWARDS PHASE OUT

By the time the U-2R was introduced, the small number purchased by the Agency and its dwindling C model fleet made the viability of maintaining separate operations increasingly questionable. Their main operational tasks were providing Det H aircraft on Taiwan for Project TACKLE and the mobile deployment capability through Det G. A significant amount of Det G's time was spent in a technical evaluation of colour film for reconnaissance use, in conjunction

with the NRO, known as 'Red Dot'. It started in the late 1960s and continued as commitments permitted. An exhaustive process, Red Dot evaluated possible uses, quality issues, the use of photographic filters and comparisons of black and white with colour imagery. The outcome of the many test flights was a detailed technical report in 1972.[1] However, this and several other minor projects can largely be regarded as 'fill in' or 'make work' tasks.

Experimental polka dot paint scheme. The reason for painting the aircraft in this way is unclear. (CIA)

This looks to be the first version of the NCR 'Magic Paint' trial in June 1969. The stripes were bright green colour on the ground but intended to change significantly as the temperature dropped. The second trial resulted in a more extensive repaint. (CIA/Roadrunners)

Invisible Aircraft

Making the U-2 less visible at high altitude had long been a subject of attention for U-2 project staff. The original highly reflective silver finish was soon superseded by a blue-black, that gave way to the familiar black finish intimately connected with the U-2. There was the application of early radar-absorbent paints to the 'Dirty Bird' aircraft in 1957–1958. Indeed, after the 1960 Powers loss, there was a short-term return to the natural metal finish to re-establish an 'air of innocence' to U-2 activities.[2] The US Air Force went further and used grey paint schemes for its HASP flights and mixed pale blues applied for the ALSS test deployed to the UK in 1975. This was specifically intended to make a distinction between CIA U-2 'spyflights' and the USAF's rather different activities.

Later some efforts saw polka dots applied to the upper surface reportedly to make it less visible to aircraft from above! Better documented are some 1969 flights to test a 'magic paint' developed by the NCR company. The paint changed colour according to the U-2's skin temperature. The changes were unlikely to be even, as temperatures across the airframe varied considerably. For example, hot closer to the engines and coldest on the wing surfaces next to the fuel tanks. The initial tests in August 1969 were said to be quite disappointing. For the second series, more comprehensive preparations were made. Art 383 (N805X) had areas of its paintwork stripped back and two different primers applied with the 'magic paint' over key areas of the aircraft. Thermocouples measured the aircraft skin temperatures in places. After take-off the U-2 rendezvoused with two T-33s at 30,000ft. They took pictures and collected 'other' data. The U-2 then climbed to a representative operational altitude for a period to 'cold soak'. It then descended to meet up with the T-33s again for further pictures and data collection

Table 4: extract from the 1972 TACKLE U-2R training programme[5]		
Duration	**Training**	**Location**
1½ weeks	Pre-training physical examinations	San Antonio, TX
1 week	Pre-training interviews, suit fittings	Washington DC
8 weeks	Language training	Los Angeles, CA
1½ weeks	Mountain/desert survival	Sierra Mountains
1½ weeks	Jungle training, water survival, drown proofing	Florida
3 weeks	T-37 Ground/flying training	Edwards North Base
1 week	Physiological training	Edwards North Base
2 weeks	U-2R ground training	Edwards North Base
10 weeks	U-2R flying training	Edwards North Base
30 weeks approximate total		

while the U-2's airframe was still cold. The results of the second set of tests on 30 October 1969 were said to be more encouraging. A post-flight report described how:

> [The] second look at 35,000 feet after the cold soak showed all colours darker and no variance between aileron/wing. No apparent temperature gradient was observed across the paint thickness.
>
> When viewed from 300 yards behind and below it could be seen the outer wings were lighter in colour and merged better with the sky background at that altitude.[3]

TACKLE Continues

Regular missions began again in May 1968 and continued until May 1974.[4] An extract from the 1972 TACKLE U-2R training programme details the main elements of the US course before the pilots returned to Taoyuan to become operational. Whilst at Edwards the students were kept largely separate from 1130th ATTG staff, except those instructing them, and away from most other base facilities.

On their return to Taiwan, the pilots began flying operational peripheral missions. They were a mixture of H camera-equipped or Long Shaft SIGINT fit flights. When the H camera was unserviceable, or otherwise unavailable, the emphasis of missions would shift to the

Table 5: Det H U-2 Peripheral Missions around the PRC[6]									
Year	1968	1969	1970	1971	1972	1973	1974	Total	
	6	12	14	20	36	25	9	122	

Long Shaft system. The 40 Committee authorised up to four SIGINT and four photographic missions for most months, though rarely were all flown. There were also specific 'blackout' periods when PRC peripheral missions were prohibited, normally when high-level diplomatic and political meetings were scheduled between US and PRC representatives. Table 5 illustrates the annual operational peripheral missions conducted by Det H.

The British at Edwards AFB

After the rapid withdrawal of the RAF pilots from Adana in May 1960, the RAF's now renamed JACKSON programme continued but in a far less active way. Two British pilots were assigned to U-2 operations at a time. They were not used operationally but flew occasional ferry flights and maintained their training currency. British MoD records identify the U-2 training programmes for RAF pilots assigned to JACKSON. The 1963 RAF Pilot Training Programme is shown in Table 6.

Table 6: The 1963 RAF Pilot Training Programme	
Duration	Training
2 weeks	Medical evaluation and pressure suit fitting
22 weeks	SAC U-2 conversion at Laughlin AFB
2 weeks	Escape and evasion and resistance to interrogation training
4 weeks	Conversion to U-2C at Edwards AFB
1 week	In-flight refuelling training
4 weeks	Initial carrier landing training (T-2A Buckeye)
35 weeks total	

Several JACKSON pilots successfully trained for aircraft carrier operations. That involved some 20 hours flying US Navy T-2A Buckeyes and 20 cable landings before they were considered for full carrier qualification by landing a U-2 on deck.[7] The training programme was amended when all conversion training switched to Edwards and the introduction of the U-2R.

Several Saints

In the years when Det G was not deployed on contingency operations, it tested its mobility commitment through a series of exercises mostly under the unclassified name of 'Scope Saint'. In the latter half of the 1960s, RAF St Mawgan hosted several of these brief deployments. UK basing of the U-2s had remained a very sensitive topic for the British government from 1956, and after 1960 was virtually taboo. Whilst the UK was supposed to be a partner in IDEALIST, their reluctance to provide basing opportunities, particularly during crises, severely limited the UK's contribution to the programme.

A U-2G (Art 348) arrived at RAF Upper Heyford after dark on 29 May 1967, having routed from Edwards via Loring AFB, supported by a KC-135A and four C-141As. A small number of training flights were planned, but international politics intervened when war in the Middle East became imminent. The deployment code-named 'Scope Panic' was hastily changed to 'Scope Safe'. Preparations escalated with the possibility of deploying the U-2G to a US Navy aircraft carrier in the Mediterranean. Instead, the Americans decided to quietly withdraw the aircraft and it returned to the US on 9 June 1967. One of the key points from the Agency after-action report was that the support arrangements had become too elaborate to move an aircraft quickly to a forward base. It advocated the need to return to the original Fast Move concept, of 20 to 25 personnel and one support aircraft for the briefest periods, with extra support for longer duration operations.[8]

After the 1967 exercise, the Americans and British worked to improve the efficiency of the operation. A May 1968 survey looked at RAF bases outside the UK that could be used for future operational deployments. Luqa in Malta, El Adem in Libya, Akrotiri on Cyprus and Masariah in Oman all met the requirements. Later RAF Gan, in the Indian Ocean, was added to the list. However, the CIA wanted to secure British agreement to contingency use of UK mainland bases again. RAF and CIA representatives worked to prove the facilities and ground equipment available at RAF airfields was adequate to support any future operation without having to bring in large amounts of extra equipment. The CIA wanted to avoid the use of USAF facilities so that questions were not asked about all the 'civilians' that would turn up to support U-2 missions. Both returned to their cover story of a joint high altitude meteorological research programme to justify the use of RAF bases.

The next exercise, Scope Saint I, took place in October 1968, involving a U-2C, KC-135A and some 40 personnel. The deployment routed from Edwards AFB, stopped over at Loring AFB and crossed the Atlantic direct to RAF St Mawgan. The Cornwall base was selected for a combination of reasons. Its location on the British west coast meant U-2 movements, including the planned simulated reconnaissance flights over the eastern Atlantic, could be accomplished largely without flying overland. As an RAF Master Diversion Aerodrome, it was open 24 hours a day and consequently carried a wider than average array of ground handling equipment. St Mawgan was regularly used by large numbers of transient aircraft from several NATO states passing through for training and exercises, so it was felt that the U-2s would not stand out too much, especially as they were to be hangared when not in use. Finally, although the region was visited by large numbers of summer holidaymakers, in spring and autumn it was comparatively quiet. Such was British sensitivity about IDEALIST, that they ruled out the logical use of RAF Wyton as a potential U-2 operating location. MoD and RAF officials asserted that using the Cambridgeshire airfield might draw unwanted attention to the station, home to British airborne Comet C.2R, Canberra intelligence-gathering and photo-reconnaissance operations. Whilst in Britain the CIA's U-2 'drivers' were styled as USAF Lieutenant Colonels, but in the event of a serious accident would have been described as Lockheed company pilots. The RAF pilots reverted to wearing their uniforms again, which they did not at Edwards AFB. Whilst at St Mawgan they were scheduled to fly two four-hour-long simulated photo-missions, clockwise, around the west coast of Ireland and back to base. The British insisted the CIA aircraft carry US national markings, which ironically even USAF U-2s did not at the time.[9]

Det G quickly adapted a detailed and periodically updated 'mobility plan' for the rapid launching of different scales of deployed operations, as directed by their project headquarters. This followed the lines of the old 'Fast Move' concept and the deployment locations ranged from pre-surveyed airfields to wholly new ones. In 1969

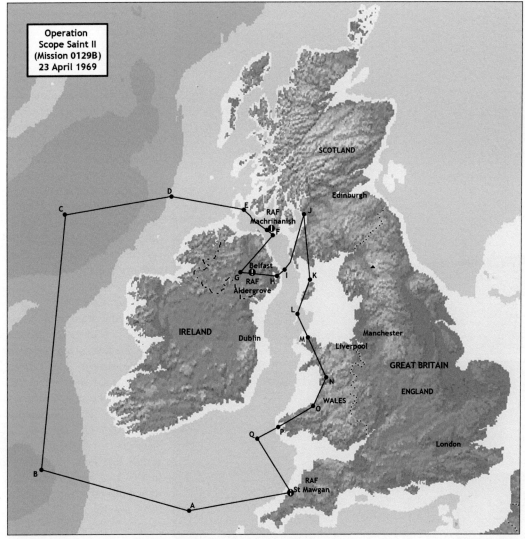

Scope Saint II was the first deployment of the U-2R to the UK. Mission 0129B took in targets across the UK having flown around the Republic of Ireland. (Map by Tom Cooper based on Landsat/Copernicus, Data SIO, USN, NGA, GEBCO, USGS and GeoBasis-DE/BKG)

C-130 as required. Their first simulated mission (0119B) was to be flown on 18 April with a B camera, carrying 4,000ft of film. It climbed to a 72,000ft penetration altitude after leaving St Mawgan and followed a similar clockwise route around Ireland. Targets along the track included Islay airport, Port Ellen in Scotland, RAF Machrihanish, RAF Aldergrove and Belfast's industrial area, Ayr and RAE West Freugh airfield in Scotland, Douglas and the Isle of Man. In Wales, it was to overfly the Menai Bridge on Anglesey, RAE Llanbedr and RAF Brawdy. The RAF was considering the possibility of placing the B camera in a Canberra PR.9 and wanted imagery from this mission for evaluation.

However, events did not go entirely as planned. Only one RAF pilot deployed because the other was diagnosed with mumps just before departure. On the first evening, Art 053 was parked in a hangar at St Mawgan where a forklift, owned by the US Navy detachment there, struck the U-2's wing. Repairs required a new aileron, which was immediately flown over from the US. Quickly

plans were updated to cover the different support requirements of the U-2R.

A Phase I deployment involved 'the movement of a forward detachment to a preselected site with one U-2R aircraft and the minimum personnel and equipment required to perform one reconnaissance overflight mission'. A Phase II deployment would be slightly larger in terms of personnel and equipment, to enable a single U-2R to perform five or six reconnaissance missions, over 30 days. A Phase III deployment could involve one or more U-2Rs and 'the necessary personnel and equipment required to sustain one U-2R for 90 days or two for 45 days' at a forward location.

The mobility plan contained very detailed packing lists of equipment required for different U-2R sensor configurations and missions. So, there were 'kits' for aircraft carrier and bare base operations and different kits to suit B, D, IRIS/IRIS II and H camera use. There were additional packages such as those to enable engine changes and for independently developing tracker camera imagery, at the forward base.[10]

The April 1969 Scope Saint deployment to the UK, was significant because it involved the first use of the U-2R. It followed similar lines to the previous operation. U-2R Art 053 was due to be flown by Squadron Leader Dick Cloke, accompanied by a C-141A support aircraft crossing with it. Their stay at St Mawgan was to last from 17 to 26 April. The necessary JP-7 fuel was delivered by USAF

completed, 053 flew a one-hour air test on 21 April followed by two training missions on 23 and 24 April. This included the planned photographic flight, now identified as mission '0129B' and used the callsign 'Flood 32'. The planned departure home on 25 April was delayed by excessive crosswinds and 053 finally left the following day, direct to Edwards AFB, flown by the RAF pilot and took 13 hours five minutes, an astounding feat for an un-refuelled jet flight.

The photographic mission produced only around 120ft of B camera film (about 75 useable frames) and was returned to the UK by an RAF VC-10 in June, after processing in the USA. A summary of the photographic material revealed some interesting information on its quality. The resolution was as high as just six inches, in high contrast line situations – such as white lines on roads – up to three miles either side of the route, sometimes down to individual lines on tennis courts, or objects one foot square. The 1L/1R camera resolution at 15 miles was one to two feet on high contrast subjects and three feet square for objects. At 25 miles distant, line detail was discernible at five to six feet and 12 feet square objects.[11] The flights had also used their System VI SIGINT equipment which provided data tapes of radar transmissions from around the UK and Ireland.

Scope Saint III was a short deployment consisting of two training missions on 22 and 24 October 1969 to an officially undisclosed location but understood to be RAF Kinloss. At short notice, a T-39A was sent by HQ USAFE on 27 October 1969 to pick up the

It was usual for the larger U-2R model to fly to operating locations. However, the aircraft could be disassembled and made air-transportable in the back of a C-141. (Lockheed/CIA)

using specially developed dolly racks.[15]

Back to the Med

In August 1970 the Israeli–Egyptian war of attrition, was continuing across the Suez Canal, with significant losses on both sides. To try and avert a full-scale conflict, a temporary ceasefire arrangement took effect on 7 August 1970 and the US government decided to deploy U-2Rs to the region. They were to monitor the agreements implementation and oversee the pull-back of troops by 32 miles on each side of the Suez Canal.

The Americans approached several countries around the Mediterranean for a suitable airfield. The Turkish government was requested to permit the use of Incirlik, the Greeks for Thessalonica and Italy for Aviano or Sigonella. Although the British had long had a stake in the U-2 programme they were still reluctant to make bases available for operations. Despite Cyprus's ideally placed position at the eastern end of the Mediterranean and the presence of its Sovereign Base Areas, the British had previously been unwilling to make RAF Akrotiri available for US operations. So, it was perhaps surprising that the UK government reversed policy and offered to host two Det G U-2s at the British base. Rapid discussions took place between the US State Department and the British to put the arrangements in place.

unprocessed film taking it to Wiesbaden, for processing by the 497th RTS.[12] Scope Saint IV went to RAF Kinloss in July 1970. During the ferry flight to the UK, RAF pilot Dick Cloke had a spacer in the base ring of his helmet fail as he turned his head. It locked his helmet in position so he had to continue looking partially left for the remainder of the flight. Fortunately, he landed safely. Training flights on the missions by Dick Cloke and Harry Drew collected more useable imagery than the previous year, for further B camera evaluation.[13] Repeat practice deployments saw another U-2R and C-141A visit St Mawgan, from 18 to 28 October 1971, for Scope Saint V. It was scheduled for two training missions with the U-2R marked with the false serial '68-7333'.[14] Scope Saint VI went to RAF Wattisham for two training sorties in 1972. For rapid deployments, it was possible to disassemble the U-2Rs and move them inside a C-141A Starlifter,

Whilst SAC was unable to mount a rapid deployment to the region, the CIA did just that. The 40 Committee authorised the deployment on the afternoon of 7 August 1970. The first Det G aircraft arrived in Cyprus just 71 hours after the order to deploy for Operation Even Steven, using the well tested Fast Move plan. Two RAF pilots were to ferry the U-2Rs to Akrotiri via RAF Upper Heyford. Whilst everything was being readied for departure, at the last moment, the British withdrew permission for the use of their pilots. That meant veteran Agency pilots Marty Knutson and Bob Ericson had to ferry the two U-2Rs across the Atlantic. The slight problem was that Knutson had already flown a five-hour test mission earlier in the day. The two aircraft flew over together accompanied by their C-141A support, with Knutson supplied with a liberal quantity of caffeine pills and frequent radio check-ins to ensure he did not fall asleep for the 12 hour 30 minutes flight. The second leg of the ferry flight from Upper Heyford saw the first aircraft, flown by Jim Barnes, forced to enter the Mediterranean over Gibraltar on 9 August, as both France and Italy denied overflight clearance. The second aircraft was flown by Dan Wright and followed the next day. The first aircraft had overflown the Canal Zone, before landing at Akrotiri. Given the U-2's afternoon arrival time over the Canal Zone, the U-2's images of the Egyptian side were being taken into the sun and 'most of the results of the mission were all but unreadable. And, the Israelis who understood the light was bad for the pictures of the Egyptian side of

Table 7: 'Even Steven' Suez Canal U-2R overflights 1970[21]			
11 August	8 September	28 September	30 October
14 August	10 September	6 October	1 November
18 August	13 September	10 October	4 November
22 August	18 September	15 October	5 November
27 August (x2)	21 September	18 October	6 November
3 September	24 September	23 October	7 November
6 September	27 September	27 October	10 November

the canal assumed, we were taking pictures of their side'. As a result, the Israelis 'complained vehemently'. That saw the mission planned for the next day cancelled because of the ongoing arguments with the Americans.[16]

A 10 August 1970 State Department telegram to Tel Aviv, instructed the US Ambassador to inform Israeli General Aaharon Yariv (head of Israeli military intelligence) that the US wanted

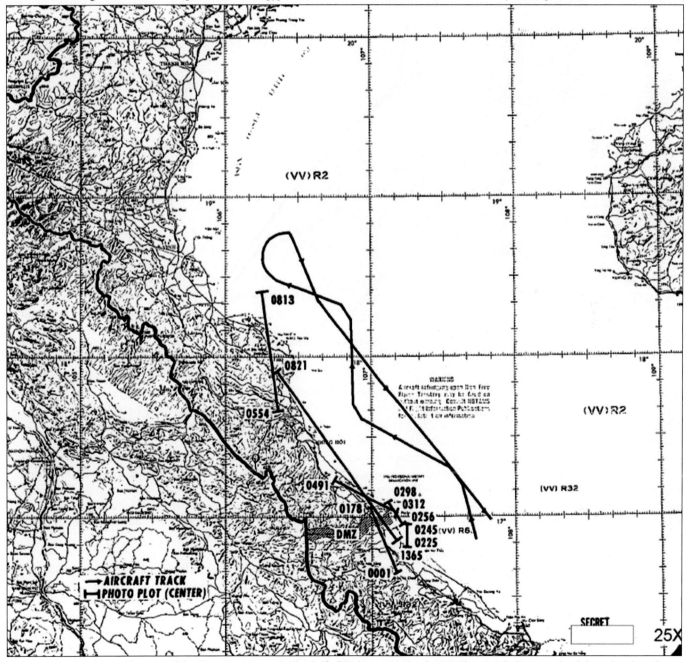

S013E map shows the U-2R's route off the Vietnamese coast in the Gulf of Tonkin on 30 March 1973. The straight lines overland show the photo line or 'PFFL'. Neither that nor the following days' flight provided good quality imagery. (CIA)

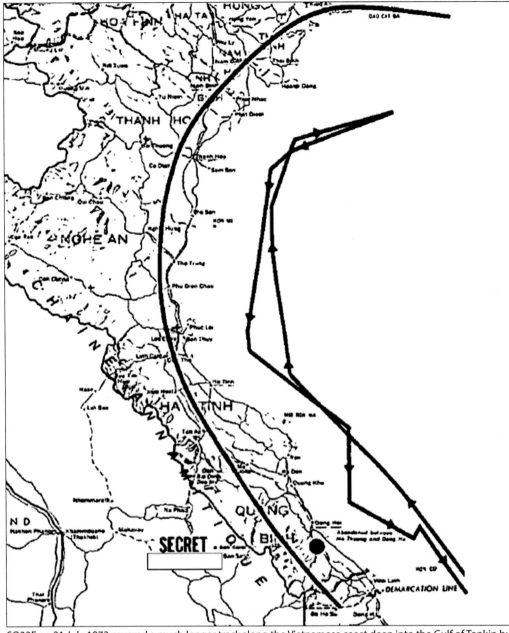

SO33E on 21 July 1973 covered a much longer track along the Vietnamese coast deep into the Gulf of Tonkin but produced little useable imagery. (CIA)

1. To cover adequately the Egyptian cease-fire zone it is necessary to have photography taken with both high and low-resolution cameras. The low-resolution photography is necessary to cover the whole area but it can only identify the more general features of suspected SAM sites and usually not the more specific details which reveal such important facts as status (ie operational or not) and type of occupancy. High-resolution photography is therefore taken to make up for these inadequacies, but it covers a much smaller area.

2. Most of our photography is low-resolution and taken at a wide-angle from the U-2s. In addition to the resolution limitation, the obliqueness of the U-2 coverage is another limitation since the farther away the target is the less detail we are able to identify and even then not all the area can be adequately covered in each flight. We can monitor most developments fairly well up to about 10 miles from the canal but beyond that, the quality begins to taper off significantly. We have begun using a new higher resolution camera with the U-2 but again this presents the dilemma of being able to identify more detail but covering less area. Many gaps can be at least partially filled by using a combination of regular high and low-resolution U-2 coverage, supplemented by periodic high and low-resolution satellite coverage.

3. There are a variety of other technical problems. These include such things as weather near the ground, upper atmospheric conditions, terrain features and the condition of the film and its development. The human analytical factor also plays a big role since many of these points are highly debatable even for highly trained photo interpreters.[18]

to work closely with them on these U-2 flights, with a 'common objective'. The Ambassador informed the Israelis that the US would provide a minimum of four hours' warning of each mission launch and provide entrance and exit times from the Sinai. It also undertook to process imagery 'as quickly as possible' and supply copies to a designated Israeli representative at their Washington embassy.[17] This was part of broader efforts to smooth Israeli feelings towards the US, who were somewhat put out that the Americans had rather foisted the agreement on them. The first full mission took place on 11 August 1970.

A State Department telegram reveals a contemporary appreciation of the limitations to imagery for the U-2's B and H cameras and satellite imagery. As it explains:

Photographic intelligence can tell us a great deal but, despite all the technical sophistication that goes into this kind of analysis, it is far from being a highly developed art and has some important limitations. There are two main types of problems:

Partway through the operation Art 053 replaced Art 055, which was sent home for planned maintenance. Between 11 August and 10 November 1970, the U-2s completed some 29 mixed SIGINT and photographic missions before they were pushed into withdrawal. The overflights had never sat comfortably with the Egyptians. On 24 November 1970, they protested to the US State Department, alleging the Americans were passing imagery from these missions to the Israelis.[19] The over 14-hour return flights to Edwards AFB from

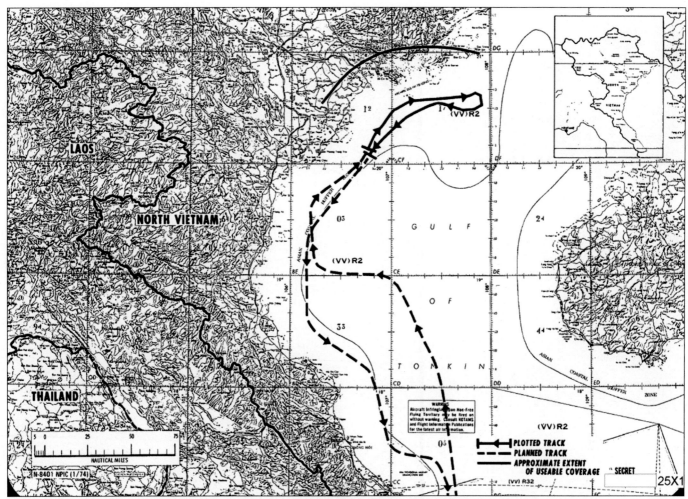

S014E was the final and most successful mission on 5 January 1974 against a perennial target, Haiphong harbour. (CIA)

RAF Upper Heyford took place on 14 December, by RAF pilots Dick Cloke and Harry Drew. These missions from Cyprus were the final operational flights by Marty Knutson, Jim Barnes and Bob Ericson, the last remaining U-2 pilots from the originals who had started flying CIA U-2s in 1956.[20]

Vietnam Peace Accords

Part of the Paris peace agreement between the US and Vietnamese governments that entered into effect during January 1973, ended the long-running war between the two countries and prohibited US military overflights. Instead, under the training deployment code-named 'Scope Shield' four Agency missions were surreptitiously launched from Taoyuan, using Det H aircraft and US crews as an attempt to monitor North Vietnamese compliance with the agreement. The four flights were mounted between widely spread dates and used the Detachment's H camera.

The first flight, S013E, was on 30 March 1973 piloted by Dave Young. To avoid PRC radar detection these missions saw the aircraft take off and fly at very low-level until they closed on the target area. Part of the mission report states: 'The photographic interpretability was significantly degraded by haze, obliquity and scale. No new intelligence was obtained by the mission. The aircraft's track remained approximately 20nm from the North Vietnamese mainland.' Photographic 'highlights' included the Ben Hai pontoon river crossing that marked the division between North and South Vietnam. Dong Hoi airfield was imaged from some 33.5nm away. Although the runway was visible no other activity was discernible. In the 'Finger Lakes' area, six known SA-2 sites were imaged, but significant detail could not be interpreted.

Flown on a parallel track, 20nm from the Vietnamese coastline, S023E, the second mission, was on 31 March 1973. It imaged an area slightly further north than the first. It included Dong Hoi airfield again, but this time was close enough to identify two Li-2 (C-47 Dakota type) aircraft parked there, around 33nm distance from the U-2R's H camera. The image quality was again said to be affected by haze, distance and problems with image processing.

S033E was flown on 21 July 1973 and followed a much longer route from abreast the Quang Tri province in the South to the Do Son peninsula in North Vietnam. Again, the imagery was sub-optimal because of haze, angle, distance plus vegetation masking objects. Targets, such as vehicles, were said to be identifiable by type at 20 miles but beyond that additional problems with the H camera's focus prevented most identification analysis.

The final mission of the series S014E was flown on 5 January 1974 and was the most successful, with much more encouraging imagery. It had been scheduled for the previous autumn but was postponed when Operation Forward Pass saw the two Det G aircraft and pilots moved forward to the UK, during the Yom Kippur War.[22] Although it passed along the Vietnamese coast, its primary photographic goal was around Haiphong harbour, from around 36nm away. A one-off waiver granted on 10 August 1973 by the 40 Committee, allowed the U-2 to fly closer to the islands opposite Haiphong harbour and enabled much better imagery to be collected of the main port area.[23] From Mission S014E, the unique design of some of the larger vessels in Haiphong harbour meant they could be identified. Distance and masking prevented clear identification of the many small vessels, individual buildings and loads sitting on the dockside, although railway rolling stock could be counted. The aircraft experienced

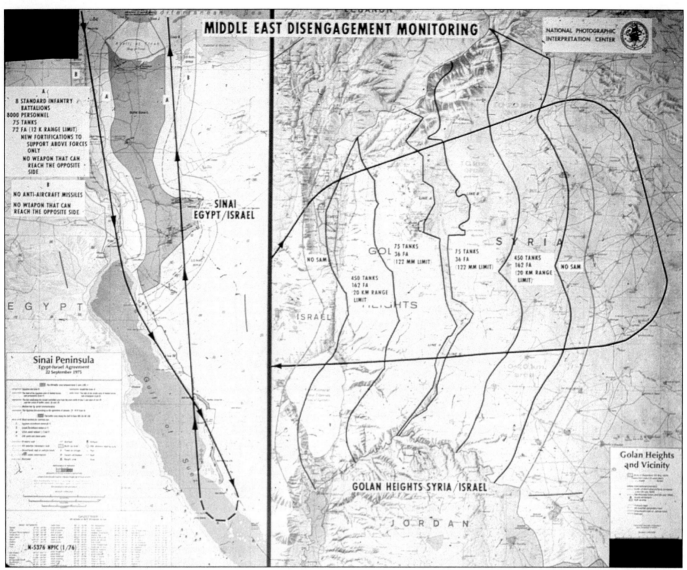

NPIC chart showing Olive Harvest route over disengagement monitoring zones in the Sinai (left) and Syria and the Golan Heights (right). The point of entry was over Port Said, down to the town of Suez, along the demarcation line for Egyptian forces. It then reversed northwards covering the demarcation line for Israeli forces back into the Mediterranean and on to Syria. Initially, the two routes were flown separately but were later merged into a single flight. (NPIC via AF Historical Foundation)

a flameout during its descent phase heading home but the pilot managed an airborne restart.[24]

Operation Forward Pass

During the October 1973 Yom Kippur War, the US wanted overhead imagery of the conflict and prepared Operation Forward Pass. With just four U-2Rs in the CIA inventory, it put major strains on both Detachments G and H. Det G moved two aircraft forward to RAF Upper Heyford. Art 055 departed for the UK on 7 October with Art 054 following the next day. It was just the sort of event the British and Americans had jointly exercised over the previous few years with the Scope Saint exercises. The British were reluctant to permit a U-2R mission from the UK, mainly in the face of dire economic threats from the Middle East OPEC states. In any case, it would have had to fly via Gibraltar again and recover to Akrotiri in the absence of French transit permission. Art 054 remained at Upper Heyford until it returned to the US on 17 October.

The British had also refused permission for SR-71A basing in the UK. Once SAC completed a Blackbird Middle East overflight, direct from the continental US on 2 November 1973, the urgent necessity declined somewhat. Meanwhile, Art 055 remained in the UK until 13 November 1973, just in case a mission was ordered.[25]

Det H was using Arts 051 and 053 during 1973. It was down to one operational aircraft during the period of Forward Pass. Art 051 was in Long Shaft configuration, whilst Art 053 had been sent to Edwards AFB to help with further H camera evaluation. Key components from its H camera had been removed in September 1973 and sent to the US for factory level 'mirror installation and thermal modifications' and so Art 053 had no operational capability during that time.[26]

Olive Harvest

After the Yom Kippur War, the Syrian, Egyptian and Israeli governments agreed to US overflights of the area, to confirm the removal of specified forces from designated disengagement zones, as detailed in the ceasefire agreements. Post-war the initial overflights were flown by SR-71s, but the task was soon passed to the U-2 as a more viable long-term option.

This time the British quickly agreed to the use of RAF Akrotiri as the U-2 base but insisted that Cypriot President Makarios give his assent to the operation. Even though Egypt's president Sadat was firmly against publicly acknowledging the overflights, the U-2's presence was deliberately made public, rather than allowed to gradually leak out, as it had in 1970.[27] In late April 1974 U-2R

Art 055, flown by Jerry Shilt, arrived at Akrotiri for what became Operation Olive Harvest. Between 12 May and 28 July there were six overflights of the disengagement areas. Flights began initially just over the Sinai, but following a US request, the British agreed to extend its use, to allow flights over Syria after 29 June 1974.[28] Initially, flights over the two areas were conducted separately, but later at least some coverage of both areas was combined into single missions.

Whereas the 1970 missions were navigationally relatively straightforward (following the line of the Suez Canal) the entry and exit points were now more complicated, using lines defined by the temporary ceasefire. This later solidified in the Sinai Agreements, and the U-2 observation flights also included a route over the Golan Heights. Flights were originally scheduled every 7 to 10 days, with the parties and the UN Force able to request additional missions. The US was to make the imagery available to the state parties and the UN Force Commander. Missions were notified 24 hours in advance and established a two-hour window for penetration of Israeli and Egyptian airspace. The Americans selected the imagery to be shared.[29] Precise navigation was challenging, particularly over the Golan Heights. Early overflights attracted protests from the Syrian government, sensitive to even minor course deviations as they were very suspicious of the arrangement pushed onto them.

However, Agency involvement in operations from Cyprus would prove short-lived. On 1 August 1974, the CIA's remaining U-2s and responsibility for the mission were handed over to Strategic Air Command. Art 055 was signed over to the 100th SRW, whilst forward deployed in Cyprus. The 'Olive Harvest', mission over Sinai and the Golan Heights was to be a 'temporary' task in 1974 but continues to this day under USAF control.

Reorganisation and Phase Out

During August 1969 there were recommendations from the 303 Committee that the U-2 was no longer necessary because of the new SR-71, constantly improving satellite imagery, and the D-21 'Tagboard' drone (ultimately unsuccessful) meant the U-2's capabilities could be dispensed with. Arguments around its flexibility with the ability to quickly deploy and a variety of sensors were the main reasons put forward by the CIA for its retention. In December 1969 those arguments won the day, backed by President Nixon and Henry Kissinger, and ensured the U-2 would continue at least until 1971.[30] However, investment in the IDEALIST programme dropped significantly and from then on was under almost continuous review, with the ultimate intention to terminate the programme.

The administration was sufficiently impressed by the speed of the Agency's 'Even Steven' deployment to Cyprus, that they wanted to retain the capability. However, continued Agency operations were to be subjected to further review by the 40 Committee. It was becoming clear that the CIA's U-2 control was unlikely to continue much longer. A large number of factors were drawing together to ensure the programme's eventual termination. The CIA was undergoing a significant internal reorganisation, plus there was extra congressional scrutiny as the Watergate scandal unfolded. The existence of a separate, small number of Agency U-2Rs that could easily be absorbed by the Air Force U-2 programme, was becoming increasingly difficult to justify. The most important single factor working against closure was the TACKLE agreement with the nationalist Chinese. The value of the TACKLE to the US was declining too, as relations with the PRC were rapidly improving, indeed continued operations with Taiwan were becoming politically embarrassing as a result. However, the withdrawal of Det H was difficult to do without their concurrence and risked alienation of

this extremely supportive ally. Another programme extension was granted by the 40 Committee in August 1972. In March 1973 the US renegotiated a key section of the Razor agreement with the nationalist Chinese, that permitted either side to terminate it with just three months' notice. In June CIA Director James Schlesinger confirmed to the 40 Committee that this significant obstacle to TACKLE and IDEALIST's closure had been removed. On 30 August 1973, the 40 Committee accepted the CIA's plan to terminate the programme by 1 August 1974 and along with it closure of the CIA's Office of Special Activities.[31]

TACKLE and JACKSON Closure

Once the phase-out decision was made at the US government level and an approximate date set, the CIA notified the Taiwanese and British governments that their involvement would also end. On 1 April 1974, the US Ambassador in Taipei informed the nationalist government of the American intention to close the TACKLE operation. In June 1974 there was a formal US notification of Det H's closure set for 23 July 1974. Peripheral H camera and Long Shaft missions had been continuing, but when the notification arrived at Taoyuan the final operational mission had already been flown. This was C194C on 24 May 1974, a photographic flight, to the Dalian (Port Arthur) area, flown by Qiu Songzhou. The Det H closure date was not announced locally until 23 July 1974 by the unit manager Warren Boyd and CIA withdrawal preparations were immediately actioned. A few days later the two U-2Rs (Art 051 and Art 053) were

In 1969, Liyi 'Jack' Chang was released from close custody and briefly returned to his home town of Nanjing. He had not seen his mother for 27 years. The nationalist government refused to allow him to return to Taiwan when he was released in 1982. He subsequently went to the US, aided by the CIA until finally allowed to return to Taiwan in 1990. (https://www.xuehua.us/a/5eb5da4986ec4d63e69f3b80?lang=zh-tw)

DETACHMENT H ON TAOYUAN

Official images of the U-2s used by Det H are difficult to locate. In the detachment's final month of existence there were some last opportunities for photographs before everything ended. A small number of images from that time have reached the public domain that give us a tiny glimpse of the aircraft and crews at Taoyuan in June and July 1974.

Tucked away on the eastern side of Taoyuan airfield was Det H's fenced compound. The hangar held two U-2s accessed via doors to the front and rear of the site. When closed, the gates and eight feet high fencing made it impossible to see through. The 55-gallon drums were used to carry the fuel for deployed operations. (Taiwan MND)

Sitting in the Taoyuan compound, speed brakes out, the folded wingtips of the U-2R can be seen. In the background is the Detachment's Cessna U-3A used for light transport and passenger movements. (https://blog.xuite.net/tomschen/blog/587560575, accessed 10 March 2021)

U-2R 053/10331 was serving with Det H when the order to withdraw was given and was ferried home, along with Art 051 by Agency pilots Tom Leshan and Jerry Shilt. This was the third of the initial U-2R order that had folding wingtips. (https://blog.xuite.net/tomschen/blog/587560575, accessed 10 March 2021)

The last six Taiwanese U-2 pilots trained for the U-2R, along with Warren Boyd. From left to right: Qian Zhu, Yi Zhiqiang, Qiu Songzhou, Warren Boyd (Det H Manager), Shen Zongli, Wei Cheng, and Cai Shengxiong. (Taiwan MND)

For local use, Det H maintained a U-3A in standard USAF 'Blue Canoe' markings. When TACKLE terminated the aircraft, 57-5859 was passed to the ROCAF. Re-serialled 3601 it remained in service until 1981 and now resides at the ROCAF Museum at Gangshan. (Fred Willemsen)

flown by Det G pilots Tom Leshan and Jerry Shilt from Taoyuan back to Edwards AFB.[32]

Termination of the JACKSON operation was much simpler. The main direct programme input consisted of two British pilots, a doctor and support personnel at Edwards AFB. Kelly Johnson and Lockheed were similarly notified of the change in late June and the transfer of CIA U-2 assets to the Air Force by 1 August was outlined.[33]

Trying to assess the Det H pilots' achievements is as complex as their range of activities was diverse. Certainly not all the outcomes were tangible. On at least two occasions their missions had helped defuse fears of a PRC invasion of Taiwan. The regularity of their flights probably also prevented additional unnecessary invasion scares. Their overflights had revealed details of the PRC's nuclear programme, charted airfields, missile sites and other key military–industrial locations that were otherwise beyond reach. TACKLE managed to record them until comprehensive satellite coverage reached maturity. Similarly, it enabled a look into significant portions of the Chinese hinterland that showed, just as in the Soviet case, that they were militarily empty spaces. The Chinese use of SAMs against U-2 flights focussed the development of better radar, missile warning and countermeasures, especially against the ubiquitous SA-2. We can only speculate what the international consequences would have been if a CIA pilot, rather than a Taiwanese one, had

flown these missions and been brought down over the PRC to be put on trial in Beijing.

The courage of the Taiwanese U-2 pilots over the years cannot be doubted, although their activities incurred high personal costs. Of the 28 Taiwanese U-2 pilots from 1961 to 1974, six died in accidents, three were lost on overflights (plus two more captured) and another killed during a peripheral mission.[34] When TACKLE closed in 1974 Det H had flown approximately 102 overflights up to 1968 and around 122 peripheral missions between 1968 and 1974.

The British

Following the British pilots' evacuation from Det B in May 1960, their role became much more limited. Real operational tasks were not found for them. They mostly flew ferry and test flights and kept their currency on the T-33A and U-3A 'Blue Canoes'.

Of the 13 RAF pilots that flew the U-2 during OLDSTER and JACKSON, most came from a fighter background, having operationally flown Lightnings or with test pilot and ETPS experience. They went on to varied careers following their period flying the U-2. At least two later reached Air Officer rank. They revealed very little about their 'black' experiences, even to other RAF colleagues. Ivor 'Chunky' Webster, with his test flying experience, was so valuable to the U-2 programme, that the Americans persuaded him to stay and he adopted US citizenship. In 1971 he joined NASA, at their Ames

U-2 Pilot No	Rank	Name	First U-2 Flight Date	Notes
93	Flt Lt	John MacArthur	3 June 1958	
94	Flt Lt	David Dowling	4 June 1958	
95	Flt Lt	Michael Bradley	10 June 1958	
96	Sqn Ldr	Christopher Walker	12 June 1958	Died in U-2 crash 8 July 1958
103	Sqn Ldr	Robert Robinson	29 September 1958	
155	Sqn Ldr	Ivor Webster	9 March 1961	
156	Sqn Ldr	Charles Taylor	13 March 1961	
187	Sqn Ldr	Martin Bee	18 June 1964	
188	Sqn Ldr	Bazil Dodd	19 June 1964	
238	Flt Lt	Richard Cloke	12 January 1968	
251	Flt Lt	Harry Drew	1968	
271	Sqn Ldr	Ian McBride	1971	
276	Sqn Ldr	Ron Shimmons	13 May 1972	

Table 8: RAF pilots trained to fly the U-2[35]

Research Centre, to continue flying the two 'ER-2s' transferred from the USAF. Webster was joined there by other veteran CIA U-2 pilots, Jim Barnes and Bob Ericson. Marty Knutson, one of the first CIA U-2 pilots, was appointed as NASA's programme manager.

Olive Tree

The CIA's withdrawal from the U-2 business did not bring operations to an end. Indeed, the now USAF Olive Harvest missions

from Cyprus soon provided a convenient cover for other U-2 activities in the region. During 1975 the British acceded to an American request to use RAF Akrotiri for SIGINT fit U-2R missions around the Syrian, Egyptian and Israeli coasts. The initial 90-day trial would be used to transmit the in-flight data collected from the U-2 to Akrotiri and then on to the US via satellite. This was the 'Senior Spear' COMINT collection system. As they would also benefit from the US sharing of the collected data, GCHQ and the Defence Intelligence Staff firmly supported the idea and British approval was given on 10 April 1975, under the code name Olive Tree. The operation probably went largely unnoticed alongside the Olive Harvest monitoring missions.[36] The flights were over international waters, at varying minimum distances of 74 to 206 nautical miles off Syria, and 68 to 110 miles off Gaza and Egypt. In May 1975 the programme consisted of a flight every three days, from 1 May then another ten in June.[37] In July the US formally sought an indefinite extension to the 'Olive Tree' operation with the British.[38]

CONCLUSION

The termination of Agency U-2 operations was an inevitable but anti-climactic ending to what had been, just a few years previously, a groundbreaking, advanced technology-packed programme. It had reached high into the atmosphere. It had carried astounding optical and electronic sensors, to collect intelligence over some of the world's most secret and inaccessible areas. The U-2 had amazing performance but required skill to fly and was difficult to handle. Yet still, men took it into great danger and several paid the highest personal price doing just that. Sometimes they achieved major intelligence coups, often they did not, but the simple fact that they regularly reached into the stratosphere to fly missions, often reassured friends and allies. It perhaps encouraged enemies to exercise more caution, lest their activities were quickly discovered, seen and recorded potentially for the world to see. Such achievements rested on the courage of one man at a time, sitting in a cramped cockpit, doing near-impossible things.

Collectively what U-2 pilots did significantly helped to calm nerves in times of great tension, helping to replace the unknown with greater clarity and certainty. The greatest achievements of CIA U-2 operations were not just what they did, but when they did it. This included searching for missile and bomber gaps over the USSR in 1956, flying over the Sino-Indian frontier, the Cuban missile crisis and over Arab-Israeli ceasefire zones in the 1970s. These were occasions when Cold War tensions were high (for different reasons) and there were few alternative means available to collect the intelligence required. The CIA's U-2s were able to cover virtually

any crisis area in the world at just a few days' notice when necessary. No other system, not even satellites, could achieve that.

Assessing the successes and failures of the CIA U-2 programme starts with a recognition that it was all underpinned by huge amounts of ambition, innovation and determination to succeed. Simply the imagination to design an aircraft that could fly so high and successfully operate in the mid-1950s is often overlooked today but remains astounding. That it was done so quickly is even more remarkable and must be to the great credit of Kelly Johnson, Lockheed, Edwin Land and the teams of scientists and engineers that worked on the early stages of the programme.

The U-2 was an aircraft packed with advanced, often ground-breaking, optical and electronic technology. It was often so advanced that the line between success and failure was very thin and frequently it dipped into failure, especially in the very demanding conditions of the upper atmosphere. This was particularly so for the early electronic SIGINT systems. They were heavy, most were failure-prone, subject to electronic interference from other equipment on the aircraft, and the data they produced was difficult to record and interpret. However, most of these systems gradually advanced, some quicker and more successfully than others. Reliability and capabilities improved as the science and technology developed, sometimes it was the U-2's immediate operational requirements that drove further innovation.

The A camera series worked well, but it was the B camera that became synonymous with the early photographic successes of the

U-2. However, we should not forget that it too, especially early on, was affected by the vagaries of mechanical failures, as was the very sensitive photographic film used, sometimes caused by human error and at others, simply by the effects of extreme cold at high altitudes. The quality of stand-off LOROP photography, even with the H camera, never met expectations. Unable to adequately overcome issues of image stability, sharp focus, or the effects of haze and clouds, it never matched the clarity of overhead imagery until the advent of the OBC narrowed the gap. Indeed, it was only from the 1990s onwards and well into the current century that electro-optical imagery and synthetic aperture radars have produced high-quality LOROP imagery.

One outcome of packing all this advanced aerodynamic, photographic and electronic technology into a single platform meant equipment failures were frequent. Sometimes equipment faults were life-threatening, others via warning lights just notified the pilot that a piece of equipment had failed, about which he could do nothing. Other times the failure was not known until after the mission was completed and the photographic or electronic 'take' processed. As a result, many missions were cancelled or delayed, aborted in-flight, only partially successful or perhaps even totally wasted, with no end product at all.

Predictably it was weather, principally heavy cloud or high adverse wind speeds, that caused the most mission delays and failures. Many were delayed by days; sometimes even entire mission series were cancelled due to prolonged periods of bad weather. Adverse conditions for departure, or anticipated during a mission, caused lots to be cancelled. Many others found the weather over their targets much worse than anticipated. Forecasting was made all the more difficult because the weather information that was necessary for successful missions over the target areas was far beyond observation, deep inside the USSR or PRC. All the SAC forecasters could hope to benefit from were intercepts of actual weather observations as they were transmitted around the Soviet Union which they then used to assemble their own weather forecasts.

One seriously overlooked area in most analyses of U-2 performance is just the pressures on airframes and pilots at times. The small, combined CIA/USAF purchase of only 55 U-2As had declined to just 13 airframes between 1956 and 1969, a loss rate averaging over three aircraft per year. To that must be added those situations (and there were lots of them) when aircraft were damaged in less serious accidents, but still required substantial repair work at the Lockheed plant. Airframes often had to be returned to the continental US from overseas detachment bases and operating locations, for flight-hour based maintenance checks and essential modifications. Managing those rotations was a major logistical headache. There were often substantial numbers of one-off projects and updates going on at any time, especially in the early years. Modifications such as the Project Rainbow aircraft, the System VII installation and fitting the U-2 aerial refuelling equipment, all further reduced overall airframe availability. Fortunately, many modifications were done at the detachments by Agency, Lockheed and contractor personnel. This was essential if a credible operational capability was to be maintained.

As if these factors alone did not significantly affect aircraft and crew operational availability, we must add essential training commitments. Training new pilots caused peaks in aircraft demand, to which can be added the hours required to maintain the currency of existing pilots. All were affected by and had a cumulative effect on airframe availability.

Keeping the U-2 and its pilots safe from being shot down was a high priority. The two principal threats were from aircraft and missiles; these have already been covered at length. In the early years of operations neither was an immediate threat to overflights. Fighters could not reach the operational heights achieved by the U-2s and early air-to-air missiles were inadequate for the task. Similarly, surface-to-air missiles were not an immediate issue in 1956. However, the USAF and Agency were well aware that the U-2 was operating in a rapidly closing gap, as air defences successfully reached ever higher. The level of threat was regularly reassessed and U-2 safety extended well beyond the original estimates of mid-1957. The employment of careful routing, warning systems and deception methods intended to avoid direct clashes with Soviet and Chinese air defences, pushed the fateful date further back still. However, judging the exact time when a U-2 would be brought down was only ever going to be by caution, luck or tragedy. So it was until May Day 1960.

We know that U-2 was demanding to fly at the best of times, but in difficult conditions its narrow performance envelope and comparative fragility could make it impossible to recover from some situations and resulted in significant losses and fatalities. Basic analysis shows some 30 U-2s were lost during training or testing related flights from 1956 to 1969, resulting in 18 fatalities. This figure includes losses due to equipment failures, such as the problems with the pilot's oxygen system. In July 1958 that led to the deaths of Squadron Leader Chris Walker and Captain Al Chapin Jr. Although the U-2 was normally safe from fighters at usual operational altitudes, its propensity for engine flameouts was worrying. The engine could not be restarted until it descended to a much lower altitude, well within fighter reach. That problem took time to resolve.

Moving to the operational use of the U-2, we enter a situation where boldness and caution had to be balanced. Bold in terms of the tasks and situations in which the U-2 and its pilots were called upon to perform collecting imagery or SIGINT. Cautious in terms of calculating the risks to which aircraft and pilots were exposed. This was much more about politics and policy. The politics, at least until May Day 1960, was about denial and obfuscation. Denial about what the capabilities of the aircraft were, obfuscation about where it was operated from and just how extensive those operations were. Keeping a low profile, operating with as much secrecy as possible, certainly helped the CIA to continue U-2 flights after 1960, as after that they rarely made front-page news.

Justifying U-2 overflight operations was a question that presidents, heads of intelligence agencies and the Joint Chiefs of Staff had to address. At its most blunt, overflying other countries' airspace could be construed as an act of war. If U-2 missions were unlikely to trigger war, did its operations amount to adventurism? They were certainly bold, but not reckless. Always carefully planned and most with clear objectives intended to meet a perceived urgent and immediate intelligence need. The potential gain had to be balanced against the risk and there was no other platform anywhere near as capable as the U-2 until the A-12/SR-71 flew, and even it experienced similar vulnerabilities.

The risk to men and machines could be significantly reduced if missions could be performed without anyone noticing. However, that suffered an immediate blow when the very first flights over Eastern Europe and USSR in 1956 were detected and mostly tracked by the Soviets, even though air defences were then impotent against them. Against many other states, especially those in the Middle East between 1958 and 1960, their activities went largely unnoticed, as they did against some areas of East Asia. Whilst in private the Soviet Union well knew who was mounting this systematic overflight programme against them, how should it respond? In secret, the Soviets began an immediate crash programme to extend and strengthen their air defences. To simply publicly protest all the violations risked looking weak and unable to defend its borders. This accounts for why many protests about U-2 airspace violations were made privately.

The US policy of 'plausible denial' worked, superficially at least, until there was concrete proof of culpability. This was another reason why Gary Powers' loss on May Day was so significant. The Americans had not expected the wreckage of his U-2 to be as complete as it was, or for him to survive. The inaccurate assumption made, was that the U-2's wreckage would amount to nothing identifiable by the time it hit the ground from over 60,000ft and the pilot would almost certainly be dead, which led to the belief that they could sustain continued denial. However, in the immediate wake of Powers being shot down, the US denials had continued. Even after the Soviets produced irrefutable evidence, the denials continued for a while and looked even more ridiculous. Subsequent overflights of the PRC using the Taipei government as a proxy gave the Americans sufficient political distance that their involvement with Detachment H operations had little international or domestic political effect, even when it sustained numerous losses.

Was the CIA the right organisation to manage the U-2 programme? Certainly, with the great benefit of hindsight, it was. It was applauded for developing the U-2, given it had never handled a complex aircraft development programme before. Kelly Johnson, Lockheed and lots of other highly technologically skilled people managed those tasks. However, the immense organisational skills of Richard Bissell certainly overcame the many other obstacles that emerged, as this unique, highly secret, project advanced. What Bissell and the CIA brought to the task was organisational agility. It was a much smaller organisation and, unlike the US Department of Defense, was not so blindingly bureaucratic, or constantly trying to juggle multiple competing interests. The Agency had significant funds that it could move to where they needed them, without having to engage heavily with the congressional budget process. It was an organisation already experienced at working in great secrecy in the far corners of the world. The Agency successfully set up U-2 detachments, albeit not according to the plan originally envisaged, with the aid of the US State and Defense Departments. They persuaded a few countries to host detachments, or permit staging operations, often traded in for a quid pro quo of a policy concession, military assistance or development aid. The CIA deployed its aircraft much more quickly, with a smaller, simpler and quieter footprint than the US Air Force could have managed.

In assembling this text and trying to cover all the many accomplishments of the CIA's U-2 programme, one factor still stands head and shoulders above all the others. These are the U-2's 'drivers'. The courage of the Agency, Taiwanese, USAF and British U-2 pilots, to repeatedly go alone, above remote, desolate parts of the world and often, knowingly, into great danger, remains outstanding. They no doubt had a very practical view of the missions they flew, intent on getting airborne, reaching their objectives and returning safely with images secure on photographic film or signals on magnetic tape. It must have been incredibly frustrating for them when things did not go according to plan. No matter if it was high over Moscow, the Himalayas, the Chinese nuclear plant of Lanzhou, the jungles of South East Asia or the deserts of the Middle East, trying to successfully navigate using a drift sight, find gaps in the cloud and avoid enemy fighters and missiles, remain remarkable accomplishments. They were on the edge of the atmosphere, the darkness of space above them and the features of the earth far below, coaxing along a fragile aircraft supported by only two thin wings, a single engine and protected only by a thin pressure suit and an oxygen mask. They collected intelligence in a way no one else on earth could do. Doing that repeatedly took great skill and courage.

Table 9: CIA and SAC U-2A/U-2R Production, Attrition and Disposition 1956–1974

U-2A production	CIA	SAC	Total
Original	20	30	
USAF additional order 1958		5	55
U-2R production			
Original	5	7	
USAF additional order 1981–1989		37	49
Total			104

Table 10: Annual U-2A to U-2G and CIA U-2R attrition by Art no. and variant

1956	Dates of loss	Pilot fatality	End of year remainder
345A	15 May 1956	Billy Rose	
354A	31 August 1956	Frank Grace	
346A	17 September 1956	Howard Carey	
357A	19 December		51
1957			
341A	4 April 1957	Bob Sieker	
366A	28 June 1957	Lieutenant Leo Smith	
369A	28 June 1957	Lieutenant Ford Lowcock	
361A	26 September 1957		
371A	22 November 1957	Captain Benny Lacombe	46
1958			

Table 10: Annual U-2A to U-2G and CIA U-2R attrition by Art no. and variant

380A	8 July 1958	Squadron Leader Chris Walker RAF	
365A	9 July 1958	Captain Al Chapin Jr	
364A	6 August 1958		
364A	6 August 1958	Lieutenant Paul Haughland	
377A	11 September 1958	Captain Pat Hunerwadel	42
1959			
(no losses)			42
1960			
360C	1 May 1960		
387A	14 July 1960		40
1961			
351C	19 March 1961	Major Yaohua Chih ROC	
353A	14 September 1961		38
1962			
376A	2 January 1962		
344F	1 March 1962	Captain John Campbell	
378C	8 September 1962	Lieutenant Colonel Huai Chen ROC	
343F	27 October 1962	Major Rudolph Anderson	34
1963			
355C	1 November 1963		
350F	20 November 1963	Captain Joe Hyde Jr	32
1964			
356F	22 March 1964	Captain Thepei Liang ROC	
362G	7 July 1964	Lieutenant Colonel Nanping Lee ROC	
395A	14 August 1964		
370E	18 September 1964	Major Robert Primrose	
379A	18 December 1964		27
1965			
358C	10 January 1965		
382G	26 April 1965	Buster Edens	
352C	22 October 1965	Lieutenant Colonel Chenwen Wang ROC	24
1966			
372F	17 February 1966	Major Tseshi Wu ROC	
342F	25 February 1966		
363A	22 March 1966		
384C	21 June 1966	Major Chingchang Yu ROC	
386C	28 July 1966	Captain Robert Hickman	
390C	8 October 1966		
391A	17 October 1966		17
1967			
375A	1 July 1967		
373A	8 September 1967	Captain Lungpei Hwang ROC	15

Table 10: Annual U-2A to U-2G and CIA U-2R attrition by Art no. and variant

1968			
394C	31 May 1968		14
1969			
385G	5 January 1969	Major Hsieh Chang ROC	13
1970			
057R	24 November 1970	Major Chi Hsien Wang ROC	12
1971			
392C	18 November 1971	Captain John Cumney	
CIA U-2Cs remaining August 1974		4	
USAF U-2Cs remaining August 1974		8	
CIA U-2Rs remaining August 1974		4	

Table 11: Original CIA U-2s transferred to SAC in August 1974 and eventual disposal

347F	Display NASM
348G	Display NASA Ames Research Centre
349G	Display Museum Warner Robins AFB
359F	Display IWM Duxford

Table 12: CIA U-2Rs transferred to SAC August 1974

	Dates of loss	Pilot fatality	End of year remainder
051R			
053R			
054R	15 January 1992	Captain Marty McGregor	
055R	22 May 1984		4

Table 13: Original SAC U-2A/C still active 1974 and eventual fate

367C	29 May 1975	Crash
398C		Display SAC Museum
374E		Display Laughlin
381C	31 January 1980	Crash
383C		Display
388D		Display
389A		Display
393A		Display

End of year totals based on total 55 U-2A purchased even though
final deliveries not completed until March 1959.
Sources for all of the above: CIA CREST and Pocock, *50 Years of the U-2*, pp.406–409.

False serial numbers were often applied to CIA and USAF U-2s, to deliberately mislead and confuse. This is a slightly different case. U-2C Art 390 with its 'correct' USAF 56-6690 serial. It crashed in April 1966. However, it was not the first aircraft to be allocated that serial number. That was U-2A Art 357 which was delivered to the CIA on 21 September 1956. It crashed soon after, on 19 December 1956, flown by Bob Ericson. Thankfully he escaped safely and went on to be one of the Agency's most successful U-2 'drivers'. (CIA)

BIBLIOGRAPHY

Bergin, R., 'The Growth of China's Air Defences: Responding to Covert Overflights 1949 to 1979', *Studies in Intelligence*, 57:2 (June 2013), pp.19-28

Bishop, R., *Shady Lady: 1,500 Hours flying the U-2* (Manchester: Crecy, 2017)

Brugioni, D., *Eyes in the Sky: Eisenhower, the CIA and Cold War Aerial Espionage* (Anapolis: Naval Institute Press, 2010)

Caddell, J.W., 'Corona over Cuba: The Missile Crisis and the Early Limitations of Satellite Imagery Intelligence', *Intelligence and National Security*, 2016, 31:3, pp.416–438, DOI: 10.1080/02684527.2015.1005495

CIA, CREST: *Utility Flight Handbook*, March 1959, <https://www.cia.gov/library/readingroom/docs/DOC_0005729692.pdf>

CIA, Directorate of Science & Technology, *History of the Office of Special Activities from Inception to 1969*

DTIC, *High Altitude Sampling Programme* (Washington DC, DASA,1961), <https://apps.dtic.mil/dtic/tr/fulltext/u2/267616.pdf>

Fletcher, R.D. Smith, J.R., & Bundgaard, R.C., 'Superior Photographic Reconnaissance of Tropical Cyclones', *Weatherwise* (1961), 14:3, pp.102–109

Garver, J.W., *The Sino-American Alliance: Nationalist China and American Cold War Strategy in Asia* (London: Routledge, 1997)

Hersh, S.M., *The Samson Option: Israel's Nuclear Arsenal and American Foreign Policy* (London: Random House, 1991)

Hua, H., *Lost Black Cats*, (Bloomington, IN: Authorhouse, 2005)

Hua, H., 'The Black Cat Squadron', *Air Power History*, 49:1 (Spring 2002), pp.4-19

Jackson, M., Clifford, G., Hoffman, G. and Ackerman, D., 'A Parameterization of the ltek, KA-80A Panoramic Camera'. *Photogrammetric Engineering and Remote Sensing*, 48:5, May 1982, pp.761–769

Israel Ministry of Foreign Affairs, 'Sinai II Accords', *Israel's Foreign Relations: selected documents, 1974-1977*, Ed. Medzini (Meron, Jerusalem: Ahva Press, 1982)

Merlin, P., *Unlimited Horizons*, (NASA: Washington DC, 2015)

NRO-CSNR, *BRIDGEHEAD: Eastman Kodak Company's Covert Photo-reconnaissance Film Processing Programme* (Chatilly,VA: NRO-CSNR, 2014)

Pedlow G., and Welzenbach, D., *The Central Intelligence Agency and Overhead Reconnaissance: The U-2 and Oxcart Programs 1954-1974* (New York: First Skyhorse Publishing, 2016)

Pocock, C., *50 Years of the U-2: The Complete Illustrated History of the "Dragon Lady"* (Atglen PA: Schiffer Military History, 2005)

Reade, D., 'U-2 Spy Planes: What You Didn't Know About Them', *Air Power History*, 58:3 (Fall 2011), pp.6-15

Richardson, R.L., *Spying from the Sky* (Oxford: Casemate, 2020)

Richelson, J., *Spying on the Bomb* (New York: WW Norton, 2007)

Santucci, J., *The Lens of Power: Aerial Reconnaissance and Diplomacy in the Airpower Century* (PhD Thesis, Maxwell AFB, 2013)

Spanberger, L., *Our Mission Revealed* (Bloomington, IN: Xlibris Publishing, 2014)

Stanley, R., *Asia from Above* (Bloomington IN: Authorhouse, 2014)

USAF, *AF(C)-1-1, U-2C and U-2F Flight Manual*, <https://info.publicintelligence.net/USAF-U2.pdf>

Wright, K., 'Catch a Falling Star', *Aeroplane Monthly*, 48:5 (May 2019), pp.58–64

Wright, K., 'Stratospheric Cold War Warriors: Alconbury's TR-1As', *Aviation News*, 82:3 (March 2020), pp.24–28

Wright, K., *The Collectors: US and British Cold War Aerial Intelligence Gathering* (Warwick: Helion & Co., 2019)

ONLINE ARCHIVE SOURCES

Central Intelligence Agency
CIA Records Search Tool (CREST): <https://www.cia.gov/library/readingroom/>

Eisenhower Presidential Library
<https://www.eisenhower.archives.gov/>

Foreign Relations of the United States (FRUS)
State Department, Office of the Historian: <https://history.state.gov/>

UK National Archive
<http://www.nationalarchives.gov.uk/>

US National Archive
<https://www.archives.gov/>

NOTES

Chapter 1

1 CIA, Directorate of Science & Technology, *History of the Office of Special Activities from Inception to 1969*, pp.1379-1386.

2 Department of State Bulletin, 1957, <https://babel.hathitrust.org/cgi/pt?id=ucl.31158003100970;view=1up;seq=149>, accessed 28 August 2018.

3 FRUS: Memorandum for the Record, by the President's Staff Secretary (Goodpaster), 18 December 1956, <https://history.state.gov/historicaldocuments/frus1955-57v24/d65>, accessed 28 August 2018.

4 CIA-RDP61S00750A000500030115-5.

5 CIA-RDP78T04753A000100230001-7,
CIA-RDP78T05439A0003003500035-6.

6 CIA-RDP62B00844R000200080025-8.

7 <https://www.eisenhowerlibrary.gov/sites/default/files/research/online-documents/aerial-

8 intelligence/1958-04-22.pdf>.

9 Another U-2 (Art 342) flew as 'chase plane' that day piloted by Sam Snyder. His aircraft suffered a flameout and he had to make an emergency landing at Taoyuan, CIA RDP75B00349R000200220015-2.

10 Mission 6015 on 18 August was an air-abort landing back after just over three hours 30 minutes, CIA-RDP78T04753A000700010024-0, CIA-RDP78T05693A0002000100005-5, CIA-RDP89B00551R000900140025-0. These coastal flights became the main peripheral missions from 1968 up to the Detachment's closure in 1974.

11 J.W. Garver, *The Sino-American Alliance: Nationalist China and American Cold War Strategy in Asia* (London: Routledge, 1997), pp.176–77.

12 CIA-RDP89B00551R000900170001-3,
CIA-RDP89B00551R000900170002-2.

13 CIA, *History of the Office of Special Activities*, p.1401.

14 CIA, *History of the Office of Special Activities*, p.1400.

15 CIA-RDP90T00782R000100040001-9.

16 CIA-RDP63-00313A0006000030025-6, CIA-RDP62B00844R000200250001-5. RD Fletcher, JR Smith & RC Bundgaard (1961), 'Superior Photographic Reconnaissance of Tropical Cyclones', *Weatherwise*, 14:3, pp.102–109.

17 CIA-RDP89B00569R001000280001-3.

18 <https://apps.dtic.mil/dtic/tr/fulltext/u2/267616.pdf>, p.99.

19 CIA, *CREST: Utility Flight Handbook*, pp.4–40.

20 DTIC, *High Altitude Sampling Programme* (Washington DC: DASA,1961), <https://apps.dtic.mil/dtic/tr/fulltext/u2/267616.pdf>, p.71, pp.230-32, accessed 11 April 2021.

21 CIA, *History of the Office of Special Activities*, p.1404.

22 CIA, *History of the Office of Special Activities*, p.1402; Chris Pocock, *50 Years of the U-2*, p.89.

23 CIA, *History of the Office of Special Activities*, p.1407.

Chapter 2

1 Kevin Wright, *The Collectors: US and British Cold War Aerial Intelligence Gathering* (Warwick: Helion & Co., 2019), p.194.

2 CIA, *History of the Office of Special Activities*, pp.1520, 1525 and 1527.

3 CIA, *History of the Office of Special Activities*, pp.1532–1536.

4 Hsichun 'Mike' Hua, 'The Black Cat Squadron', *Air Power History*, 49:1 (Spring 2002), p.8.

5 R. Bergin, 'The Growth of China's Air Defences: Responding to Covert Overflights 1949 to 1979', *Studies in Intelligence*, 57:2 (June 2013), pp.19 and 28.

6 <https://www.nti.org/learn/countries/china/nuclear/>, accessed 11 January 2021.

7 Richelson, *Spying on the Bomb* (New York: WW Norton, 2007), pp.138–141.

8 C. Pocock, *50 Years of the U-2: The Complete Illustrated History of the "Dragon Lady"*

9 (Atglen PA: Schiffer Military History, 2005), p.136.

10 CIA-RDP89B00569R000500010011-3.

11 CIA-RDP78B04560A0004000010011-2.

12 CIA-RDP89B00569R000500010033-9.

13 CIA, *History of the Office of Special Activities*, p.1559.

14 Roy Stanley, *Asia from Above* (Bloomington IN: Authorhouse, 2014), p.179.

15 Hua, 'The Black Cat Squadron', p.8.

16 CIA CREST DOC_0001104420.pdf,
CIA-RDP78T05439A000300390028-0.pdf, <https://www.atomicarchive.com/almanac/facilities/prc-facilities.html>, accessed 13 January 2021.

17 <http://www.theworldofchinese.com/2015/02/factory-221/>, accessed 14 January 2021; <https://www.independent.co.uk/news/long_reads/china-atomic-bomb-plant-221-mao-zedong-science-research-a8171736.html>, accessed 14 January 2021.

18 Pocock, *50 Years of the U-2*, pp.138–139.

19 Hua, 'The Black Cat Squadron', p.11.

20 CIA-RDP33-02415A000300150040-7; Pocock, *50 Years of the U-2*, p.138.

21 CIA, *History of the Office of Special Activities*, p.1568.

22 Hua, 'The Black Cat Squadron', p.9.

23 CIA, *History of the Office of Special Activities*, p.1566.

24 CIA-RDP33-02415A000300150009-2.

25 Hua, 'The Black Cat Squadron', pp.8–9.

26 See Spanberger, L, *Our Mission Revealed*, for details of the AFSPPF and NRO-CSNR, BRIDGEHEAD, covering Easkman-Kodak's role.

27 Stanley, *Asia From Above*, p.57.

28 CIA-RDP61S00750A000300180037-8.

29 Stanley, *Asia From Above*, p.180.

30 Stanley, *Asia From Above*, pp.178–179 and pp.439–442.

31 CIA, *History of the Office of Special Activities*, p.1568.

32 CIA-RDP89B00569R000900140009-2.

33 CIA-RDP89B00709R000100120017-7.

34 CIA-RDP89B00709R000100120007-8.

35 CIA-RDP66B00664R000100060114-8.

36 Hua, 'The Black Cat Squadron', p.12.

37 CIA-RDP02T06408R000800010012-9;
CIA-RDP02T06408R000500010034-8.

38 Hua, *Lost Black Cats* (Bloomington, IN: Authorhouse, 2005), pp.36–37.

39 Hua, *Lost Black Cats*. This is the account of Yeh's story as a communist Chinese prisoner, written by fellow U-2 pilot Mike Hua.

40 Both Kunsan AB in South Korea and Cubi Point were used as launch or recovery staging bases for ROC U-2 operations,

although the fact is rarely recorded. Kunsan was used for some flights over North Korea. Cubi Point was used for some mainland China missions (Hua, 'The Black Cat Squadron', pp.10–11).

41 Hua, 'The Black Cat Squadron', p.12.

42 CIA-RDP66B00664R000700070013-3.

43 Hua, 'The Black Cat Squadron', p.13; CIA-RDP66B00664R000700020056-1; CIA-RDP66B00597R000100110020-1.

44 Hua, *Lost Black Cats* (Bloomington, IN: Authorhouse, 2005), pp.125–131.

45 CIA-RDP77B00403R000100010005-1.

46 Hua, 'The Black Cat Squadron', pp.13 and 16.

47 CIA, *History of the Office of Special Activities*, pp.166, 1442, 1561, 1579 and pp.1633–1646.

48 Author communication with Lieutenant Colonel Rick Bishop.

49 CIA, *History of the Office of Special Activities*, pp.1509–1510.

50 CIA-RDP89B00709R000100180006-3; CIA-RDP89B00709R000100180007-2.

51 CIA-RDP89B00709R000100180009-0.

52 CIA-RDP78B04558A000900040116-1.

53 <https://beyondparallel.csis.org/tag/yongbyon-declassified>, <https://beyondparallel.csis.org/yongbyon-declassified-part-ii/>, accessed 9 April 2021.

54 KH-4 missions: 9050 (15 December 1962), 1008 (15 July 1964), 1023 (17 August 1965).

55 <https://www.cia.gov/library/readingroom/docs/DOC_0001471954.pdf>. The major intervals in coverage were caused by temporary halts to missions following losses of TACKLE aircraft.

56 CIA-RDP66B00597R000400020009-1; CIA-RDP66B00597R000400020002-8.

57 CIA, *History of the Office of Special Activities*, p.1583.

58 17 February 1966 (Art 372) Major Tseshi Wu and 21 June 1966, (Art 384) Major Chingchang Yu.

59 CIA-RDP68B00724R000100070005-9; CIA-RDP71B00590R000100050032-6.

60 CIA, *History of the Office of Special Activities*, pp.1612–13.

61 CIA, *History of the Office of Special Activities*, p.1592; Hua, 'The Black Cat Squadron', p.16.

62 CIA-RDP74B00776R000100030043-0.

63 CIA, *History of the Office of Special Activities*, p.1784; CIA-RDP71B00263R000100060090-4; CIA-RDP71B00263R000100060032-8.

64 CIA-RDP71B00263R000100030083-5.

65 Hua, 'The Black Cat Squadron', p.16.

66 Hua, 'The Black Cat Squadron', p.16.

67 CIA-RDP71B00263R000100080021-8; CIA-RDP68B00724R000200090023-6; Pocock, *50 Years of the U-2*, pp.246–252.

68 CIA, *History of the Office of Special Activities*, pp.1594–1599.

69 CIA-RDP78B04549A000300010004-0.

70 CIA-RDP78B04560A006400010033-2.

71 G. Pedlow & D. Welzenbach, *The Central Intelligence Agency and Overhead Reconnaissance: The U-2 and Oxcart Programs 1954-1974* (New York: First Skyhorse Publishing, 2016), pp.248–255.

72 Hua, 'The Black Cat Squadron', p.17.

Chapter 3

1 CIA, *History of the Office of Special Activities*, pp.1438–1439.

2 Richardson, *Spying from the Sky* (Oxford: Casemate, 2020), pp.188–189.

3 CIA, *History of the Office of Special Activities*, pp.1438–1439.

4 Richardson, *Spying from the Sky*, p.198.

5 CIA-RDP89B00569R000900250174-7.

6 CIA-RDP68B00255R000200110006-6, p.7.

7 CIA-RDP89B00569R000600310031-1; CIA-RDP89B00569R000600310030-2.

8 CIA-RDP68B00255R000200110005-7.

9 CIA, *History of the Office of Special Activities*, p.1448.

10 CIA-RDP33-02415A000200020004-2. More detailed coverage can be found of USAF U-2 Cuban missile crisis operations in Pocock, *50 Years of the U-2*, pp.165–180. Also in Pedlow & Welzenbach, *The Central Intelligence Agency and Overhead Reconnaissance*, pp.210–223.

11 Joseph W Caddell, 'Corona over Cuba: The Missile Crisis and the Early Limitations of Satellite Imagery Intelligence', *Intelligence and National Security*, 2016, 31:3, p.427.

12 Kevin Wright, 'Catch a Falling Star', *Aeroplane Monthly*, 48:5 (May 2019), pp.58–64; Caddell, 'Corona over Cuba', p.436; CIA-RDP78B04560A000300010033-9.pdf.

13 Caddell, 'Corona over Cuba', p.418.

Chapter 4

1 Richardson, *Spying from the Sky* (Oxford: Casemate, 2020), p.190.

2 Pedlow & Welzenbach, *The Central Intelligence Agency and Overhead Reconnaissance*, p.233.

3 CIA-RDP89B00569R000400140127-2; CIA, *History of the Office of Special Activities*, pp.1775–1776.

4 CIA-RDP89B00569R000400140122-7.

5 CIA-RDP89B00569R000100060015-2.

6 CIA, *History of the Office of Special Activities*, p.562.

7 CIA-RDP89B00569R000100230045-0; CIA-RDP89B00569R000100230043-2; CIA-RDP89B00569R000100230063-0; CIA-RDP78B04560A000200010021-3.

8 Missions: 6056, 6058, 6060.

9 U-2F conversions were Arts: 342 (prototype), 343, 344, 350, 356, 359 and 372; SAC air-refuellable U-2Es 347 (later to U-2F), 370 and 374 (later to U-2F); Pocock, *50 Years of the U-2*, pp.406–408.

10 P. Merlin, *Unlimited Horizons* (NASA: Washington DC, 2015), pp.61–63; CIA, *History of the Office of Special Activities*, p.83; CIA-RDP74B00447R000100010018-2.

11 Missions: 3201, 3203, 3210, 3213 and 3215.

12 Richardson, *Spying from the Sky*, p.214.

13 CIA-RDP89B00569R000200030049-7; CIA-RDP89B00569R000200120067-7; CIA-RDP89B00569R000200050093-6.

14 CIA-RDP89B00569R000900190017-8.

15 CIA-RDP63-00313A000500040002-1.

16 CIA-RDP78B04560A000500010089-6.

17 CIA-RDP89B00569R000200140059-4.

18 CIA-RDP89B00569R000200150035-9.

19 CIA-RDP78B04560A001600010019-1.

20 Missions: 3227, 3230, 3236 and 3238.

21 CIA-RDP63-00313A000500140115-5; CIA-RDP89B00569R000700160013-7; CIA-RDP89B00569R000700160066-9.

22 Richardson, *Spying from the Sky*, p.216.

23 CIA, *History of the Office of Special Activities*, pp.1459–1460.
24 CIA-RDP78B04560A002600010048-8.
25 CIA-RDP89B00569R000900030024-7;
    CIA-RDP89B00569R000900030040-9.
26 CIA-RDP66B00664R000500110021-1.
27 CIA-RDP66B00664R000500110007-7.
28 CIA, *History of the Office of Special Activities*, p.1459.
29 Source data: CIA-RDP68B00724R000200130026-8.
30 CIA-RDP02T06408R000300010025-0.
31 CIA-RDP02T06408R000300010009-8.
32 CIA-RDP71B00297R000300220010-5;
    CIA-RDP68B00724R000200090017-3.

Chapter 5

1   CIA-RDP80T01137A000400080001-8.
2   U-2G conversions were Art 348, 349, 362, 381, 382 and 385. Art 349 was briefly configured as the sole U-2H also fitted with aerial refuelling equipment.
3   <https://documents.theblackvault.com/documents/cia/projectwhaletale-cia.pdf>, pp. 103–108, accessed 16 February 2021; CIA, *History of the Office of Special Activities*, p.1480.
4   R.L. Richardson, *Spying from the Sky*, pp.224–226. A CIA video of the U-2Gs arrival on USS Ranger is available at <https://www.youtube.com/watch?v=0HmowN7ZbqQ>, accessed 10 November 2020.
5   CIA, *History of the Office of Special Activities*, p.1486.
6   <https://nsarchive2.gwu.edu/NSAEBB/NSAEBB184/FR25.pdf>. CIA, *History of the OSA*, pp.1482–1491.
7   CIA-RDP74B00836R000300040001-3.
8   Originally three U-2Rs were modified with folding wingtips initially. It is likely the third aircraft was Art 053.
9   Before conversion to a U-2G in 1964, Art 349 was fitted with aerial refuelling installation. It was then also briefly fitted with the carrier fit, making it the unique U-2H. The combined weight reduced its operational ceiling significantly, so the refuelling equipment was removed in 1965 creating an extra U-2G. Merlin, *Unlimited Horizons*, p.68.
10 CIA-RDP74B00836R000300190001-7.
11 Pocock, *50 Years of the U-2*, pp.257–258.
12 CIA-RDP68B00724R000200010001-8;
    CIA-RDP74B00836R000300190001-7.
13 CIA-RDP74B00836R000300190001-7, pp.14–16.
14 CIA-RDP33-02416A000400090001-5.

Chapter 6

1   Pocock, *50 Years of the U-2*, pp.238–242.
2   CIA-RDP81B00878R000100060049-7.
3   CIA-RDP89B00487R000400730032-7.
4   CIA-RDP78T05439A000500120046-7;
    CIA-RDP67B00820R000300130020-7;
    CIA-RDP79B01709A002900070014-0.
5   CIA-RDP67B00511R000100020006-3.
6   CIA-RDP68B00724R000100010017-2;
    CIA-RDP75B00285R000200120068-3;
    CIA-RDP33-02415A000800260001-3;
    CIA-RDP67B00511R000100070006-8.
7   CIA-RDP89B00980R000200150028-7.
8   CIA-RDP68B00724R000100010017-2.
9   CIA-RDP33-02415A000800260001-3.
10 CIA-RDP68B00724R000100010017-2.
11 CIA-RDP68B00724R000200230001-4.

12 CIA-RDP74J00828R000100200027-0.
13 CIA-RDP68B00724R000200230017-7.
14 For a much more detailed explanation of the KA-80A OBC see: M Jackson et al, 'A Parameterization of the ITEK, KA-80A Panoramic Camera'. *Photogrammetric Engineering and Remote Sensing*, 48:5, May 1982, pp.761–769.
15 CIA-RDP75B00285R000200120068-3;
    CIA-RDP68B00724R000200100005-4;
    CIA-RDP75B00285R000200020007-1;
    CIA-RDP68B00724R000200020030-5.
16 Wright, 'Stratospheric Cold War Warriors: Alconbury's TR-1As', *Aviation News*, 82:3 (March 2020), pp.24–28.
17 CIA-RDP99B00048R000100110006-0;
    CIA-RDP68B00724R000200200004-4.
18 CIA-RDP71B00297R000700050002-9.
19 CIA-RDP89B00980R000600080007-4;
    CIA-RDP99B00048R000100150005-7;
    CIA-RDP99B00048R000100150001-1;
    Hua, 'The Black Cat Squadron', p.17.
20 CIA-RDP75B00159R000200120072-8.
21 Hua, 'The Black Cat Squadron', p.10.
22 CIA-RDP75B00159R000100060024-9;
    CIA-RDP78B04555A000300040092-3;
    CIA-RDP78B04555A000300040063-5;
    CIA-RDP78B04555A000300050052-6.
23 Hua, 'The Black Cat Squadron', p.17;
    CIA-RDP74B00496R000100110047-5;
    CIA-RDP74B00496R000100110051-0.
24 R. Stanley, *Asia from Above*, p.181.
25 CIA-RDP78B04560A007300010007-1;
    CIA-RDP78B04560A007300010014-3.
26 CIA-RDP75B00285R000300150008-5.
27 CIA-RDP74B00496R000400010027-5;
    CIA-RDP74B00496R000200040029-2.

Chapter 7

1   CIA-RDP78B04560A007300010030-5.
2   CIA-RDP63-00313A000600060056-9.
3   CIA-RDP99B00048R000100160005-6; CIA-RDP99B00048R000100160008-3; CIA-RDP99B00048R000100160011-9; CIA-RDP68B00724R000200060030-1; CIA-RDP99B00048R000100160004-7.
4   Hua, 'The Black Cat Squadron', p.17.
5   CIA-RDP33-02415A000600050028-9.
6   (Source: CIA Mission records)
7   TNA, AIR 40/2739.
8   Pocock, *50 Years of the U-2*, p.209;
    CIA-RDP71B00263R000100170001-0.
9   TNA, AIR 40/2796; CIA-RDP68B00724R000200220019-6.
10 CIA-RDP33-02416A000400090001-5;
    CIA-RDP33-02416A000400150001-8.
11 TNA, AIR 40/2797; CIA-RDP71B00297R000700030008-5.
12 CIA-RDP68B00724R000100170016-6.
13 Pocock, *50 Years of the U-2*, p.255;
    CIA-RDP75B00285R000300150038-2.
14 CIA-RDP99B00048R000100340001-0;
    CIA-RDP99B00048R000100350006-4.
15 Pocock, *50 Years of the U-2*, pp.276–277.
16 Pocock, *50 Years of the U-2*, p.262;
    CIA, CREST: DOC_0002863361.

17 FRUS, 1969–1976, Vol 23, Arab-Israeli Dispute, 1969–1972, Doc 146, accessed 13 October 2020.

18 FRUS, 1969–1976, Vol 23, Arab-Israeli Dispute, 1969–1972, Doc 159, accessed 13 October 2020.

19 JTA Daily News Bulletin, 25 November 1970, <http://pdfs.jta.org/1970/1970-11-25_227.pdf?_ga=2.14975925.2060587526.1614858367-939526579.1614858367>, accessed 4 March 2021.

20 Pocock, *50 Years of the U-2*, p.263.

21 CIA-RDP75B00159R000100060011-3

22 CIA-RDP79B01709A000600070010-9.

23 CIA-RDP75B00326R000100210055-2; CIA-RDP75B00159R000200130021-3.

24 CIA-RDP83-01074R000300180005-4; CIA-RDP83-01074R000300180001-8; CIA-RDP83-01074R000300280004-4; CIA-RDP83-01074R000300190001-7; Pedlow & Welzenbach, *The Central Intelligence Agency and Overhead Reconnaissance*, pp.256–257; Pocock, *50 Years of the U-2*, p.275.

25 CIA-RDP75B00285R000300150008-5; Pocock, *50 Years of the U-2*, p.276.

26 CIA-RDP75B00285R000300150008-5; CIA-RDP75B00285R000200050008-7.

27 TNA, DEFE 13/986, PM Minute PM/74/14, 15 March 1974.

28 TNA, DEFE 13/986, DS8 Minute to PS/SoS, 27 June 1974.

29 Joe Santucci, *The Lens of Power: Aerial Reconnaissance and Diplomacy in the Airpower Century* (PhD Thesis, Maxwell AFB, 2013), pp.286–288.

30 CIA-RDP74J00828R000100200009-0.

31 CIA-RDP71B00399R000600210001-0; CIA-RDP33-02415A000300350007; Pedlow & Welzenbach, *The Central Intelligence Agency and Overhead Reconnaissance*, p.267.

32 Pocock, *50 Years of the U-2*, p.278; CIA-RDP33-02415A000800210001-8; CIA-RDP33-02415A000300350007-2.

33 CIA-RDP75B00326R000100270058-3.

34 <http://www.taiwanairpower.org/u2/losses.html>, accessed 21 August 2018.

35 U-2 Pilot Listing

36 TNA, DEFE 13/987, US RPF – Olive Tree – April 1975, 10 April 1975.

37 TNA, DEFE 13/987, US RPF – May 1975; DEFE 13/987 US RPF – June 1975.

38 TNA, DEFE 13/987, US U-2 SIGINT Operation at Akrotiri (Operation Olive Tree).

ABOUT THE AUTHOR

Having taught Cold War history, international security and politics at the University of Essex, Kevin Wright is a regular contributor to several UK aviation magazines. Publications have included books on Cold War aerial intelligence, articles on contemporary topics such as Bundeswehr Special Forces, Finnish Air Force F-18 operations and many others. He holds a PhD in international relations and is an experienced academic teacher and researcher. His lifelong interest in military aviation coupled with aerial photographic work makes him well qualified to examine and evaluate Cold War aerial intelligence collection.

Kevin is also the author of *The Collectors: US and British Cold War Aerial Intelligence Gathering*, published by Helion in 2019.